QUESTIONS & ANS

THE THEORY OF CATERING

EIGHTH EDITION

RONALD KINTON, VICTOR CESERANI

AND DAVID FOSKETT

Hodder & Stoughton

A MEMBER OF THE HODDER HEADLINE GROUP

British Library Cataloguing in Publication Data

Kinton, Ronald
  Questions and Answers for the Theory of
  Catering. – 5Rev.ed
  I. Title   II. Ceserani, Victor
  III. Foskett, David
  642.076

  ISBN 0–340–64781–7

First published 1978
Second edition 1984
Third edition 1989
This edition 1996

Impression number	10	9	8	7	6	5	4	3	2	1
Year			2000	1999	1998	1997	1996			

Typeset by Wearset, Boldon, Tyne and Wear
Printed in Great Britain for Hodder & Stoughton Educational, a division of Hodder Headline Plc,
338 Euston Road, London NW1 3BH by Redwood Books, Trowbridge, Wilts.

CONTENTS

INTRODUCTION

The aim of this book is to assist students in their revision by providing questions drawn from the 8th edition of *The Theory of Catering*.

Answers and page reference numbers are supplied for short questions and outline answers with page references, for longer questions. All page numbers refer to the 8th edition of *The Theory of Catering*.

The outline answers given for the longer questions are guides to the content of the answers and do not necessarily set out the format or give details of how to present the answers.

Some page reference numbers are omitted from the menu planning chapter because the questions and answers are drawn both from that chapter and the food commodities chapter. Page references could cause confusion and have therefore been omitted in some cases. The use of *Practical Cookery* could be helpful in the menu planning chapter.

Students should note carefully the wording of all questions, e.g. state, explain, describe, list etc. and formulate their answers accordingly.

The book can be recommended for students taking NVQ levels 1, 2, and 3, also BTEC GNVQ intermediate and advanced, and the examination leading to membership of the Hotel, Catering and International Management Association.

INTRODUCTION TO THE CATERING INDUSTRY

Read pp12–13 of *The Theory of Catering*.

QUESTIONS

1   Briefly define the function of the catering industry.

2   The catering industry provides (choose one)
    medical facilities in hospitals
    educational requirements in schools
    accommodation in hotels
    tourist information in resorts

3   Give a brief description of
    a a chain-catering organisation
    b welfare catering
    c contract catering

4   A hospital patient's treatment consists of:
    a skilled medical attention
    b careful nursing
    c other factors

5   List four responsibilities of a dietician in a hospital.

6   State three examples of residential establishments requiring catering facilities.

7   Give three examples of transport catering.

8   List eight ways that catering is provided to meet the needs of people in various situations. Select four of these aspects of the industry and explain who they serve, their function and operation.

9   Why is the catering industry so important in relation to the economy?

10   **a** Why is the catering industry described as a service industry?
    b Explain the function of the catering industry in all its aspects.
    c Describe in detail one of the main areas of the industry.
    d Explain why the industry has grown, and why there are many staffing problems in the industry.

ANSWERS

1   to provide food, drink and in certain sections, accommodation for all kinds of people, in various situations, at all times   *p12*

2   accommodation in hotels   *p12*

3   e.g. **b**   welfare catering; answer to include purpose – to provide a service
not necessarily profit making – working to a budget
examples – hospitals, schools, halls of residence in colleges, hostels   *p15*

4   **c**   also involves the provision of good quality food prepared and cooked to retain maximum nutritional value and presented in an appetising manner   *p15*

5   collaborating in planning menus, drawing up and supervising special diets, instructing diet cooks, advising and assisting training diet cooks, advising patients   *p18*

6   hotels, hospitals, hostels, halls of residence, retirement homes, boarding schools   *p24*

7   aircraft, ships, trains   *p25*

8   **a**   hotels, restaurants, clubs, schools, retirement homes, industrial establishments, wine bars, pubs, fast-food, colleges, luncheon clubs, the services etc., take-aways, department stores, hospitals, hostels, transport   *pp12–27*
   b   e.g. outside or outdoor catering 'ODC'
To provide catering away from the caterer's establishment
Situations e.g. agricultural sites, church halls, new buildings, private homes
Functions e.g. county shows, private parties, banquets, weddings etc.
Requirements staff e.g. flexible, adaptable, ingenious
Considerations – variety of work, careful planning, weather problems, often unknown number to cater for   *pp12–27*

9   number of people employed, contribution to national income, major role in the tourist industry   *p12*

10 **a**   provides service to
all people e.g. ages, nationalities, social class etc.
all times e.g. for 24 hours, in many cases
all places e.g. hospitals, schools, restaurants etc.

b provision of food and drink and, in some areas, accommodation for the armed forces, prisons, hospitals, residential homes, hotels, public houses, cafes etc., industry

c e.g. hospital – provides food, drink and accommodation for patients, doctors, nurses and other staff and out-patients. Special diets. Problems of service from kitchen and transport of meals. Low budget etc.

d e.g. more people with more money
>increase of tourists
>more married women at work – more eating out
>more people go abroad and return wanting different foods
>social and economic trends

staff problems e.g. many part-time staff
>language problems
>unsocial hours
>wages
>working conditions etc.   *pp12–27*

FOOD AND SOCIETY

Read pp28–43 of *The Theory of Catering*.

QUESTIONS

1 State four important factors which affect what we eat.

2 Specify how eating can develop social relationships.

3 State your own food preferences and suggest where you think they originated.

4 List eight varied places providing meals.

5 What do you understand by the word 'media'?

6 Pair the following according to their close relationships
   historical   1 Chinese restaurant
   religious   2 health restaurant
   ethnic   3 a fast (refrain from eating)
   physiological   4 burger bar
   economic   5 wedding breakfast
   sociological   6 medieval banquet

7 A gourmet is a person who eats (choose one)
   large quantities of food
   only good quality food
   only organic food
   as a vegetarian

8 Explain
   a the economic and political influences which may affect what we eat
   b in which way foods affect us physiologically and psychologically
   c how scientific developments influence what we eat

9 Does society produce the media or the media produce society? Discuss this in relation to what, where and when we eat.

10 Why is it important for a caterer to monitor trends and fashions in food and in particular the influence of the media?

ANSWERS _____

1   select from
    tastes and habits, degree of hunger, nutritional need, resources
    (time, money), effects of advertising, availability of food   *p29*

2   choose from
    eating environment provides meeting place
    develop relationships in the home
    develop relationships in school
    develop relationships at work
    at celebrations
    in business   *p29*

3   originated from parents, school, media, peer group, health needs
    etc.   *p30*

4   cafes, restaurants, hotels, in the home, pubs, canteens, service
    stations, hostels, railway buffets, on aircraft, on ships, hospitals

5   the means of communicating information e.g. television,
    newspapers etc.   *p32*

6   historical – 6   physiological – 2
    religious   – 3   economic   – 4
    ethnic   – 1   sociological – 5   *p32*

7   only good quality food   *p31*

8   points to include
    a availability of money to purchase or goods to exchange,
        government policies regarding
        i   taxation
        ii export and import restrictions etc.
            political stability
    b feel, smell, taste, appearance of food
        new foods, nutritional content
        healthy eating, additives, diets etc.
        psychologically – advertising – peer group pressure
    c e.g., microwaves, preservatives, Quorn, TVP, chill-freeze
        etc.
        research into foods/diets, medical related diseases.   *pp32–3*

9   define society and define media, explain food habits (when and
    what is eaten) in the home, school, work place, at leisure; explain
    how the television, books, newspapers etc., influence what we eat;
    give a reason(s) for any conclusions you may state   *pp32–3*

10 to produce products the consumer is going to buy
    alter menus as changes in taste demand
    monitor sales in order to stay in business

INFLUENCES OF ETHNIC CULTURES

Read pp44–54 of *The Theory of Catering*.

QUESTIONS

1 Give three reasons why it is essential to have a knowledge of ethnic cookery.

2 State three causes that have contributed to the increase in ethnic eating places.

3 Match the following
   Muslims   Vesak
   Hindus   Ramadan
   Sikhs   Holi
   Buddhists   Baisakhi day

4 Briefly explain each of the following in relation to food
   taboo, ethnic, gastronomy, physiological, kosher, additives.

5 Match the following:
   hot cross buns   6th January
   crown cake   Good Friday
   pumpkin pie   Lent
   pancakes   Thanksgiving Day

6 Orthodox Jews eat only (choose one)
   pork products, ham and bacon, koshered meat, goat meat.

7 **a** Jewish plaited bread eaten on the Sabbath is called c . . .
   b Unleavened bread served at Passover is called m . . .
   c A traditional dish served at Pentecost is c . . .

8 Couscous is made from (choose one)
   barley, wheat, rice, maize.

9 Which is the odd one out, and why?
   chollah, ceviche, chapati, tortilla.

10 What have Sushi and Condé in common? Briefly describe each.

11 Match the following with their country of origin.

Goulash	Switzerland
Lava bread	Greece
Colcannon	America
Bouillabaisse	Italy
Haggis	Russia
Gnocchi	Hungary
Sauerkraut	Mexico
Coulibiac	Japan
Rösti	Germany
Paella	France
Taramasalata	Scotland
Succotash	Ireland
Dim Sum	Wales
Tofu	Spain
Guacamole	China

12 Waterchestnuts are used in the cookery of (choose one)
Germany, China, India, Mexico.

13 **a** Select one European and one Asian country and describe a dish
from each of the countries.
  b Choose two religions and describe an example of a food or dish
affected by the beliefs of each religion.

ANSWERS

1 select from
  because of a demand by public for ethnic dishes
  many establishments serve ethnic dishes
  great variety of foods from distant places available
  enables career opportunities to be greater and
    without this knowledge, one's full potential is restricted
  helps promote racial harmony   *p44*

2 choose from
  people from overseas have opened establishments
  overseas people initially customers
  tourism has increased demand
  interest stimulated by media, particularly television
  perishable food from distant places readily available
  often offer good products at prices people can afford   *p44*

3 Muslim – Ramadan
  Sikhs – Baisakhi day

Hindu – Holi
Buddhists – Vesak   *p45*

4   taboo – foods not permitted to be eaten
ethnic – relating to foods of racial groups
gastronomy – art and science of good eating
physiological – affecting the workings of the body
Kosher – fulfilling requirements of Jewish law
additives – additions to foods e.g. to enhance, preserve   *pp44–6*

5   hot cross buns – Good Friday
crown cake – 6th January
pumpkin pie – Thanksgiving Day, USA
pancakes – Lent   *pp44–6*

6   Koshered meat   *p46*

7   **a** chollah
b matzo
c cheesecake   *p46*

8   wheat   *p49*

9   ceviche – this is a fish dish – the other three items are kinds of
bread   *p51*

10 main ingredient is rice; sushi is cooked rice served cold, seaoned
with rice vinegar with fish from Japan; condé is a sweet rice dish
from France   *p53*

11 goulash – Hungary   lava bread – Wales   colcannon – Ireland
bouillabaisse – France   haggis – Scotland   gnocchi – Italy
sauerkraut – Germany   coulibiac – Russia   rösti – Switzerland
paella – Spain   taramasalata – Greece   succotash – America   dim
sum – China   tofu – Japan   guacamole – Mexico   *pp46–54*

12 China   *p52*

13 choose varied and interesting examples of religions and countries
so as to produce a good answer; the dishes selected should be
clearly described
a e.g. European country – Spain – paella
rice dish with shellfish, chicken, vegetables and saffron
simmered in stock and oil in a paella pan
Asian country – China – Peking duck
specially bred ducks basted with a honey mixture then roasted
and served with Chinese pancakes
b e.g. Christian – pancakes and Lent; Christians mark Lent by
fasting and therefore use up all perishable goods   *pp46–54*

FOOD COMMODITIES

Read pp56–192 of *The Theory of Catering*.

Meat

Read pp57–81 of *The Theory of Catering*.

QUESTIONS

1   Why is it necessary to know and understand the structure of meat in order to cook it properly?

2   What is the composition of lean meat?

3   The size of fibres in meat affects the grain and texture of the meat: true/false.

4   Name the two kinds of connective tissue.

5   The quantity of connective tissue that binds the fibres together has much to do with the tenderness and eating quality of the meat: true/false.

6   The quantity and quality of fat are important factors in determining eating quality of meat: true/false.

7   Meat is hung to (choose one)
      increase leanness, enable the blood to congeal, increase the flavour and tenderness, facilitate jointing.

8   Meat is generally hung at a temperature of
      −1°C, 1°C, 2°C, 4°C

9   Match the following
      pig   lamb and mutton
      calf   pork and bacon
      sheep   veal

10   State three points to consider when storing fresh meat.

11   List three points to consider when storing fresh bacon.

12   Describe how you would recognise good quality beef.

13   Are supplies of home produced veal obtainable all year round?

14   The quality of veal necessary for first class cookery requires a carcass of meat weighing approximately 100kg: true/false.

15 Would veal, described as pale pink, firm and moist with firm pinkish white fat, be of good or poor quality?

16 Could Britain be called a lamb eating country?

17 Although in Britain we produce much of our own lamb and mutton, from which other country do we import large quantities?

18 *Lamb* is the term given to animals not more than
    1 year old, 1½ years old, 2 years old, 3 years old.

19 Good quality lamb should have (choose one)
    lean, firm, bright red, fine grain flesh; hard, white, evenly distributed fat
    lean, soft, bright red, fine grain flesh; hard, white, evenly distributed fat
    lean, soft, dull red, fine grain flesh; hard, white, evenly distributed fat
    lean, firm, dull red, fine grain flesh; hard, white, evenly distributed fat.

20 Briefly describe good quality pork.

21 Briefly describe the two methods of curing bacon.

22 Green bacon has a milder flavour than smoked bacon: true/false.

23 *Bacon* is the cured flesh of pig specifically reared for bacon: true/false.

24 *Ham* is the hind leg of a (choose one)
    porker pig, cut square, pickled, dried and smoked
    baconer pig, cut square, pickled, dried and smoked
    porker pig, cut round with the aitchbone, pickled, dried and smoked
    baconer pig, cut round with the aitchbone, pickled, dried and smoked.

25 All hams must be thoroughly cooked before being eaten: true/false.

26 What is the food value of meat?

27 List four ways of preserving meat.

28 What is meant by *chilled meat*?

29 Name the joints of a carcass of lamb.

30 When ordering *prepared beef* from the butcher, what would be supplied if you ordered
    striploin, pony, rib-eye roll.

31 What is a prepared single chine and end of veal called?

32 What would the butcher supply if you ordered
    rack of lamb, hind of lamb, crown of lamb.

33 What would cuts across an uncut pair of best ends produce?

34 With pork, what is the difference between a *long* and a *short
    hogmeat*?

35 A suckling pig usually weighs
    6–8lbs, 8–10lbs, 10–20lbs, 20–22lbs.

36 The spare rib of pork is part of
    long loin, short loin, neck-end, middle hogmeat.

37 **a** Describe the structure of meat and list the main sources of
        supply.
    b Explain how meat is stored and the purpose of hanging.
    c Describe in detail the quality points of two of the following:
        beef, lamb, veal, bacon.
    d List the items named as offal, and explain how they are stored.
        Take two of the items and explain their quality points and how
        they are used.

ANSWERS _____

1 an expensive item of food; need to know best method of cooking,
    time required and when cooked; how jointed and carved   *p57*

2 muscles, fibre   *p57*

3 true   *p57*

4 elastin, collagen   *p57*

5 true   *p57*

6 true   *p58*

7 increase flavour and tenderness   *p58*

8 −1°C   *p58*

9 pig – pork and bacon
    calf – veal
    sheep – lamb and mutton

10 hung to tenderise, temperature −1°C, suspend on hooks, 90°
    humidity, hygienic conditions   *p59*

11 well ventilated, cold room, hung on hooks, cut bacon on trays in
    refrigerator, joints wrapped in muslin and hung   *p69*

12 lean – bright red with small flecks of fat, marbling
    fat – firm, brittle, creamy white, odourless   *p62*

13 yes

14 true   *p58*

15 good   *p58*

16 yes   *p70*

17 New Zealand/Australia   *p70*

18 1 year   *p70*

19 lean, firm, dull red, fine grain flesh; hard, white, evenly distributed
    fat   *p70*

20 pale pink flesh, white firm smooth fat, not excessive fat, skin
    smooth   *p67*

21 **a** salting and smoking – dry method
    b soaking in brine and smoking   *p69*

22 true   *p69*

23 true   *p69*

24 porker pig cut round with aitchbone, pickled, dried and smoked
                                                              p70

25 true

26 high protein, fat, vitamins and minerals   *p61*

27 salting, chilling, freezing, canning   *p61*

28 meat kept just above freezing in a controlled atmosphere *p61*

29 leg, breast, saddle, middle neck, scrag-end, shoulder, best-end *p72*

30 striploin – boned, fillet and thin flank removed
    pony – prepared fore rib no brisket, shank or sticking piece
    rib-eye roll – prepared fore rib with cartilage, muscle fat, gristle
    removed   *p62*

31 haunch of veal   *p66*

32 rack – best end split, chined and trimmed
    hind – two legs and loins uncut
    crown – cut across the saddle giving uncut pair of loin chops *p71*

33   butterfly cutlets   *p72*

34   long hogmeat – long loin, short hogmeat – short loin   *p68*

35   10–20lbs   *p68*

36   neck-end   *p68*

37   **a** lean: connective tissue – yellow, white fibres, age, tenderness
        fat: marbling, flavour
        tender cuts, tougher cuts   *pp58–9*
        lamb – England, Scotland, New Zealand, Australia
        beef – England, Ireland, Scotland
        veal – England, Scotland, Holland
        pork – England
        bacon – England, Denmark
        venison – Scotland
     b hanging to tenderise, increase flavour, −1°C temp, 90 per cent
        humidity, beef and veal up to 3 weeks, lamb and pork up to 2
        weeks, on hooks   *p59*
     c veal: flesh pink, firm, moist surface, porous bones, fat firm,
        pinkish white, kidney firm, fat covering
        bacon: stickiness, smell, rind, fat, lean   *p64*
     d liver, kidney, heart, sweetbread, tripe, brains, oxtail, tongue
        refrigerated at −1°C at a relative humidity of 90 per cent for 7
        days
        frozen – kept frozen
        oxtail: lean, no stickiness, braised, soup
        liver: appear fresh, colour, not dry, smell, smooth; ox liver –
        braised; calves – grilled – fried   *pp81–4*

Offal

Read pp81–4 of *The Theory of Catering*.

QUESTIONS

1   What is the name given to the edible parts taken from the inside of
    the carcass?

2   Name four items referred to in the previous question.

3   What is tripe?

4 The best tripe is
  honeydew, velvet, honeycomb, smooth.

5 Oxtails should be of good size, meaty and lean: true/false.

6 **a** What are the quality points of suet?
  b What is it used for?

7 From where is beef marrow obtained?

8 Give an example of how each of the following could appear on a
  menu
  lamb's kidney, calf's liver, ox kidney.

9 The food value of kidney is similar to liver: true/false.

10 The hearts of which animals are sometimes used in cookery?

11 The tongue of which animal is popular as a hot and cold meat?

12 Ox-tongues must be salted before being used: true/false.

13 *Sweetbreads* are (choose one)
  glands which when cooked are nutritious and digestible
  small balls of stuffing served with chicken
  offal obtained from suckling pigs
  glands from the pancreas and heart used for diets
  sweet tasting stomach lining.

14 Heart shaped sweetbreads (pancreas) are superior in quality to the
  neck sweetbreads: true/false.

ANSWERS _____

1	offal	*p81*
2	tripe, liver, heart, kidney	*p81*
3	stomach lining or white muscle	*p81*
4	honeycomb	*p81*
5	true	*p81*
6	**a** creamy white, brittle, dry	
	b suet paste for e.g. dumplings, meat puddings,	
	suet puddings	*p82*
7	in the bone of the leg of beef	*p82*

8	lamb's kidney – grilled lamb's kidney	*pp82–3*
	calf's liver – fried calf's liver	*pp82–3*
	ox kidney – steak and kidney pie/pudding	*pp82–3*
9	true	*p83*
10	ox, sheep or calves	*p83*
11	ox or lamb	*p83*
12	false, may be used fresh or salted	*p83*
13	glands which are nutritious and digestible	*p83*
14	true	*p83*

Poultry

Read pp85–8 of *The Theory of Catering.*

QUESTIONS

1   *Poultry* is the term which covers (choose one)
    domestic birds which are free ranging
    edible domestic birds and wild birds
    edible birds which have finished laying
    domestic birds bred to be eaten.

2   Indicate the correct poultry quality points
    the bird's breast should be plump
    the flesh should be firm
    the vent-end of the breastbone must be pliable
    the skin should be white and unbroken
    old birds have spurs and large scales on their legs

3   The flesh of poultry is more easily digested than that of butcher's meat: true/false.

4   Unlike meat, fresh poultry need not be hung: true/false.

5   Frozen birds must be kept in the deep freeze unit until required to be defrosted: true/false.

6   When defrosting birds it is best to (choose one)
    place them in warm water
    place them in cold water
    place them on the kitchen table
    place them in the refrigerator.

7   What is the smallest chicken known as?

8   Put in order of size – smallest first
      turkey, duck, quail, poussin.

9   Turkeys are available in weights from . . . to . . .

10   Give two quality points from prime turkey.

11   What is grey and white, feathered and resembles a chicken?

12   *Eviscerated* means
      plucked, degutted, frozen, portioned.

13   Chickens fed on maize are known as
      corn-fed, maize-fed, cereal-fed, range-fed.

14   a Define poultry and state its food value.
      b List five points of quality in chicken.
      c State three types of chicken and give an example of the use of
         each.
      d List three birds other than chicken used in the kitchen, give a
         menu example for each.

ANSWERS

1	domestic birds bred to be eaten	*p85*
2	all points are correct	*p86*
3	true	*p85*
4	false, fresh poultry needs to be hung for 24 hours	*p86*
5	true	*p86*
6	place in a refrigerator	*p86*
7	poussin	*p87*
8	quail, poussin, duck, turkey	*p88*
9	3½–20kg	*p88*
10	breast – large, undamaged skin	*p88*
11	Guinea fowl	*p88*
12	degutted	*p87*
13	maize	*p87*

14 a domestic birds bred to be eaten and for eggs; protein   *p85*
   b breast – plump, pliable breast bone, unbroken skin, small scales, firm flesh, white skin, smooth legs, small spurs   *p87*
   c poussin/spring, boiling fowl, medium chicken, capon roasting, stocks, soups, sauces, poêlé (pot roasting), grilling, sauté, roasting   *p87*
   d duck, guinea fowl, pigeon, turkey, goose
        roast duck, apple sauce, sage and onion stuffing, braised guinea fowl, pigeon pie, roast turkey, braised goose   *pp87–8*

Game

Read pp89–92 of *The Theory of Catering*.

QUESTIONS

1   State five quality points to look for in game birds.

2   What do you understand by the term *game*?

3   Name the two groups into which game can be divided.

4   Has game less or more fat than poultry or meat?

5   Game is easily digested: true/false.

6   Game birds and game animals are hung with their fur/feathers on: true/false.

7   What is the purpose of hanging game?

8   What are the four factors that determine the hanging time for game?

9   Place the following in order of size – smallest first
        pheasant, partridge, grouse, woodcock.

10   What is the name given to the flesh of deer?

11   Give two quality points for joints of venison.

12   Why is venison marinated before being cooked?
        to kill parasites
        to retain quality
        to counteract toughness and dryness
        to form the base of the gravy.

13   Of what significance are the ears of hares and rabbits?

14 With what are woodcock and snipe trussed?

15 **a** State the two kinds of game with three examples of each.
   b State three characteristics of game.
   c State the season for two game birds. Give four points of quality.
   d What is venison, how is it prepared prior to cooking? Give one menu example for venison and one for hare.

ANSWERS ───────────────────────────────

1 beak breaks easily, soft breast plumage, plump breast, pointed quill feathers, smooth legs   *p90*

2 wild birds and animals which are eaten   *p89*

3 furred and feathered   *p89*

4 less fat   *p89*

5 true   *p89*

6 true   *p89*

7 tenderise and increase flavour   *p89*

8 type of game, age, condition, storage temperature   *p89*

9 woodcock, grouse, partridge, pheasant   *p91*

10 venison   *p89*

11 well fleshed and dark brownish-red colour   *p90*

12 counteract dryness and toughness   *p89*

13 tear easily   *p90*

14 the beak   *p91*

15 **a**

Furred	Feathered	
venison	pheasant	woodcock
hare	partridge	snipe
wild rabbit	grouse	etc.

   b less fatty than poultry or meat, hanging is required, flavour, toughness is due to wild habitat (exhaustive exercise), season
   c grouse – 12 Aug – 10 Dec
      pheasant – 1 Oct – 1 Feb
      partridge – 1 Sept – 1 Feb
      woodcock – 1 Oct – 1 Feb

pliable breast bone, soft supple feet, firm breast, underdeveloped spurs

d flesh of deer – hung, marinated
   roast haunch of venison, Cumberland sauce
   jugged hare   *pp89–91*

Fish

Read pp92–103 of *The Theory of Catering*.

QUESTIONS

1 Which is the odd one out and why?
   haddock, herring, cod, whiting, hake.

2 What have the following in common
   plaice, brill, sole, turbot, dab.

3 The approximate loss from boning and waste in the preparation of flat fish is
   10%, 20%, 30%, 50%

4 The approximate loss from boning and waste in the preparation of round fish fillets is
   60%, 40%, 20%, 10%

5 What do halibut liver and cod liver contain?

6 State six points to be observed when purchasing fish.

7 Which vitamins are contained in fish?

8 Indicate the fish below using the following key: 'o' for oily or 'w' for white fish, 'f' for flat or 'r' for round fish.

   eel, pike, pilchard, John Dory, flounder, sprat, megrim, red mullet, bream, sea bream, bass, whitebait.

9 Gutted, flattened, salted, cold-smoked herring are called
   bloaters, kippers, buckling, smokies.

10 Which two fish are extensively farmed?

11 Name five smoked fish.

12 Is fish smoked at a temperature of 33°C or 43°C?

13 Hot-smoked fish is cured at a temperature of
    65°C–70°C, 70°C–80°C, 80°C–85°C, 85°C–90°C.

14 Explain the difference between the *London* and the *Scottish cure*, used when smoking salmon.

15 What are *buckling*?

16 Name three fish which are canned.

17 Kippers are produced from
    codling, herring, whiting, haddock.

18 Name three fish which may be smoked.

19 Caviar is obtained from
    salmon, skate, sturgeon, hake.

20 The conger eel is larger than the eel: true/false.

21 Mackerel must be used very fresh – why?

22 Name three British rivers in which salmon are fished.

23 *Rollmops* are
    pickled, rolled, sprat fillets
    pickled, rolled, herring fillets
    pickled, rolled, haddock fillets
    smoked, rolled, haddock fillets.

24 Name three fish which may be eaten smoked and which are not cooked apart from this smoking process.

25 What have the following in common?
    anchovies, eels, herring, salmon, sprats, tunny fish.

26 Which fish can be served jellied?

27 What is a salmon weighing less than 3½kg known as?

28 The sea-fish similar in appearance to salmon is
    tunny, rainbow trout, trout, salmon trout.

29 Sardines are only used when tinned: true/false.

30 Are trout fished from rivers, lakes or the sea?

31 Which fish is used for serving *au bleu*?

32 What is tuna?
    baby turbot, a very large fish, a quantity of trout, a kind of fish boat.

33 Which fish has nodules, turbot or brill?

34 Whitebait are the fry of young . . . ?

35 By what method of cookery are whitebait cooked?

36 Name the fish which has 'wings'.

37 Halibut is a white flat fish which can weigh up to
50kg, 75kg, 100kg, 150kg.

38 Which is considered to be the best of the flat fish?
plaice, Dover sole, lemon sole, witch.

39 What is the current market price of Dover sole?

40 The average weight of a turbot is
½–1kg, 1½–2kg, 2½–3kg, 3½–4kg.

41 Name three popular round sea-fish.

42 Explain what is meant by *en goujons*?

43 How can you distinguish a whole cod from a whole haddock?

44 Which of the following is easy to digest and therefore suitable for
the sick and elderly?
red mullet, herring, salmon, whiting.

45 Which is the more expensive – witch, lemon or Dover sole?

46 The texture of monkfish is
flaky loose, firm close, soft smooth, flaky firm.

47 What has eight arms, is 6–12 inches long and has a mottled skin?

48 Give three ways of cooking squid.

49 In what category are the following
crawfish, cockles, crayfish.

50 Name three types of scallops.

51 What is the purchasing unit of oysters?
singles, ½ dozen, tens, dozens.

52 Shellfish is easily digested: true/false.

53 Why is a little vinegar used in the cooking of shellfish?

54 Why, if possible, is it best to buy shellfish alive?

55 Arrange the following in order of size – smallest first
shrimps, lobster, prawn, crawfish.

56 The colour of live lobster is
       red, orange, green, bluish-black.

57 Hen lobsters are distinguished from cock lobsters by their
       broader/narrower tail.

58 From which lobster is coral obtained? hen/cock.

59 Name two shellfish which have two shells.

60 The name given to shellfish soup is
       soupe, purée, velouté, bisque

61 Which has claws, the crawfish or the crayfish?

62 There is usually more flesh on a hen crab, but the flesh is
       considered to be of inferior quality to that of the cock crab:
       true/false.

63 By what two features of the crab tail can you distinguish a hen crab
       from a cock crab?

64 Which is the odd one out and why?
       Whitstable, Chelmsford, Colchester, Helford.

65 The majority of oysters eaten in Britain are consumed raw:
       true/false.

66 When are English oysters in season?

67 Name two countries from which we import oysters during the
       summer months.

68 Name two essential purchasing points of quality for mussels.

69 Mussels may be served hot or cold: true/false.

70 Why are scallops so dirty when fished out of the sea?

71 Name two fish roes that are popular eaten on their own.

72 a Give four reasons why fish is a valuable food.
    b How may fish be grouped and what is their source?
    c How should fish be stored? Give five quality points.
    d i State the food value of fish.
       ii Specify three ways it may be preserved.
       iii Name five smoked fish.
    e When purchasing fish, state five points to be considered.
    f i Specify five methods of cooking.
       ii Select fish suitable to be cooked by each method.
       iii State how they could be described on the menu.

g i State three examples of fish which are smoked then eaten with no further cooking.

ii Give three examples of hot fish dishes suitable for serving at breakfast.

iii Give two menu examples of savouries using fish.

73 a Select two shellfish, describe their quality and purchasing points. State how they may be cooked and give a menu example for each.

b Name six shellfish other than two selected in **a**.

c Give examples of two shellfish served as a first course with menu example.

74 a Explain the differences between crayfish and crawfish.

b Describe the purchasing, storage and cooking of scallops.

c State three fish roes and explain their use.

ANSWERS

1	herring – only oily fish	*p92*
2	all flat fish and white fish	*p92*
3	50%	*p92*
4	60%	*p92*
5	oil	
6	no unpleasant smell, no discolouration, undamaged, sea slime but not sticky, purchase daily from market, delivered iced	*p93*
7	A and D	*p93*
8	eel – O pilchard – O, R flounder – W, R megrim – W, F bream – W, R bass – W, R pike – W, R John Dory – W, R sprat – O red mullet – W, R sea bream – W, R whitebait – O	*p92–3*
9	kippers	*p96*
10	salmon and trout	*p92*
11	haddock, herring-bloaters, herring-buckling, kippers, cod, eel, mackerel, salmon, sprats, trout	*p96*
12	33°C	*p96*
13	70°C–80°C	*p96*

14 London – light salting and smoking
    Scottish – stronger smoking more flavour   *p97*

15 small, whole, lightly hot-smoked herring   *p96*

16 sardine, salmon, pilchards, anchovies, tuna   *p95*

17 herring   *p96*

18 salmon, herring, trout   *p97*

19 sturgeon   *p95*

20 true   *p97*

21 deteriorates quickly   *p98*

22 Dee, Tay, Severn, Wye, Avon, Spey   *p98*

23 pickled, rolled, herring fillets   *p97*

24 salmon, mackerel, trout   *p97*

25 all oily fish   *p97*

26 eels   *p97*

27 grilse   *p98*

28 salmon trout   *p98*

29 false – also used fresh e.g. grilled   *p98*

30 rivers and lakes   *p98*

31 trout   *p98*

32 a very large fish   *p99*

33 turbot   *pp99–100*

34 herring   *p99*

35 deep frying   *p99*

36 skate   *p99*

37 150kg   *p99*

38 Dover sole   *p100*

39 check current price list

40 3½–4kg   *p100*

41	cod, haddock, mackerel, herring	*pp100–1*
42	cut in strips like gudgeon	*p101*
43	haddock has thumb mark and is lighter in colour	*p101*
44	whiting	*p103*
45	Dover sole	
46	firm and close	*p102*
47	squid	*p107*
48	fried, stir fried, baked, grilled	*p107*
49	shellfish	*p104*
50	Great, Bay, Queen	*p107*
51	dozens	*p106*
52	false	*p103*
53	to soften fibres	*p103*
54	then known to be fresh	*p104*
55	shrimp, prawn, lobster, crawfish	*p105*
56	bluish-black	*p105*
57	broader tail	*p105*
58	hen	*p105*
59	oysters, scallops	
60	bisque	
61	crayfish	*p105*
62	true	*p104*
63	broader tail, more flesh may have coral	*p104*
64	Chelmsford is not a place which produces oysters	*p106*
65	true	*p106*
66	May to August	*p106*
67	France, Holland, Portugal	*p106*
68	must be closed, large, no barnacles, smell fresh	*p106*

69 true *p106*

70 grow on sea bed *p107*

71 cod, herring, sturgeon *p108*

72 a major food source of proteins, vitamins and minerals, healthy
eating, variety in diet, digestible, variety to menu, cooked by
many methods, suitable for all meals, varied textures, taste,
appearance *p93*

   b oily fish, white: flat or round, shell, fresh water fish, sea
fished *p92*
off Iceland, Scotland, Irish Sea, English Channel, Scandinavia,
Canada, Japan, fish farms, rivers and ponds

   c fish refrigerator, just above freezing point, frozen fish deep
freeze, smoked fish in refrigerator *p93*
eyes, gills, flesh, scales, skin, smell

   d i protein: oily fish – Vit A & D, white fish in liver bones –
calcium phosphorous *p93*
      ii freezing, canning, salting, smoking, pickling *pp93–4*
      iii buckling, kippers, red herring, smoked salmon, haddock,
bloaters *p96*

   e Purchased daily, direct from market, undamaged, as required –
e.g. fillets, size, well iced, quality points *p93*

   f poaching: suprême of halibut dugléré
boiling: salmon and parsley sauce
grilling: grilled sole, parsley butter
shallow frying: fillets of plaice meunière
deep frying: fillet of cod, tomato sauce

   g i salmon, trout, eel, buckling
      ii kippers, smoked haddock, herrings, kedgeree, fish cakes
      iii haddock and bacon, roes on toast, kippers on toast, shellfish

73 a lobster: purchase live, heavy, size as required, claws
boiled, lobster mayonnaise
mussels: closed, large, smells
boiled, mussels marinière *pp103–7*

   b cockles, mussels, oysters, scallops, shrimps, prawns, scampi,
crayfish, crawfish, lobster, crab *pp103–7*

   c oysters – Whitstable natives *pp103–7*
prawns – prawn cocktail

74 a crayfish: fresh water, size 7cm, garnish or as lobster dishes
crawfish: like large lobsters 3–4lbs, no claws – long antennae,
mainly cold buffet *p105*

   b tightly closed, purchased cleaned, orange – bright and moist,
     refrigerate, fried or poached   *p107*
   c cods – smoked
     herrings – soft or hard – savouries
     sturgeon – caviar
     lobster – coral – butter and sauces   *p108*

Vegetables

Read pp108–23 of *The Theory of Catering*.

QUESTIONS

1   What is the nutritional value of root vegetables?

2   List six vegetables available all the year round.

3   Little protein or carbohydrate is found in green vegetables: true/false.

4   Name the nutrients found in green vegetables.

5   Describe good quality cabbage in four or five words.

6   Fresh green vegetables should be stored
     in the containers they are delivered in
     on well ventilated racks
     in vegetable bins
     in the refrigerator.

7   What happens to vegetables and fruits if they are not properly stored?

8   Because of air cargo transport, many fruits and vegetables are in season the whole year round: true/false.

9   Name two types of artichoke.

10   Name three types of fresh bean.

11   What are the two chief types of mushroom?

12   What is an alternative name for sweetcorn?

13   Name three types of vegetables that can be purchased in dehydrated form.

14   State four methods by which vegetables are preserved.

15 Name two vegetables available in dried form.

16 Name two popular pickled vegetables.

17 Name six vegetables available in deep-frozen form.

18 What is the difference between *cos* and *cabbage* lettuce?

19 Which group is obtainable fresh in winter?
 sprouts, celery, swedes, parsnips
 marrow, sprouts, asparagus, cabbage
 runner beans, carrots, swedes, sweetcorn
 peas, parsnips, aubergine, seakale.

20 What is another name for salsify?

21 A long narrow root plant used in soups, salads and as a vegetable is called s . . . ?

22 Mooli is
 long, white and thick
 long, red and thick
 short, white and thin
 short, red and thin.

23 How may sweet potatoes and yams be used?

24 Describe the difference between sweet potatoes and yams.

25 For what purpose are corn salad, radiccio and cress used?

26 Describe radiccio.

27 By what three names are peas eaten in their entirety known?

28 Give four uses of avocado.

29 How are squash, pumpkin, courgette and aubergine classified?

30 What vegetable may be described as resembling a fat pine cone with overlapping green edible leaves connected to an edible base?

31 Name and describe four types of fungi.

32 a State the food value of root and green vegetables and list their quality and purchasing points.
 b Explain the storage of vegetables and the method of preservation, with examples.
 c List the types of vegetables, with two examples for each.
 d Name and describe three types of mushroom. Explain how mushrooms may be used.

ANSWERS

1 carbohydrate (starch or sugar) protein
   mineral salts and vitamins   *p108*

2 mushrooms, carrots, cabbage, onions, potatoes, lettuce, cucumber,
   beetroot, watercress, leeks   *p109*

3 true   *p109*

4 mineral salts and vitamins   *p108*

5 tight, crisp, green, fresh not wilted   *p110*

6 well-ventilated racks   *p110*

7 lose quality – wither, shrink, discolour, dry out   *p108*

8 true   *p108*

9 globe, Jerusalem   *p109*

10 runner, French, broad   *p109*

11 cultivated, wild   *p123*

12 maize   *p121*

13 onion, carrots, potatoes, cabbage   *p110*

14 canning, dehydration, drying, pickling, salting, freezing   *p110*

15 peas, beans, lentils   *p110*

16 onions, red cabbage   *p110*

17 peas, sprouts, spinach, cauliflower, carrots, beans   *p110*

18 cos is long, cabbage round   *p110*

19 sprouts, celery, swedes, parsnips   *p109*

20 oyster plant   *p111*

21 scorzonera   *p111*

22 long white and thick   *p110*

23 fried, purée or as a sweet pudding   *p111*

24 sweet potatoes – long, coloured skin, orange flesh
    yam – knobbly and cylindrical   *p111*

25 in salads   *p112*

26 round, deep red variety of chicory, white ribs and bitter   *p112*

27 mange-tout, snow peas, sugar peas   *p121*

28 in salads, as a first course, as a soup, dips, garnish   *p122*

29 fruits   *p112*

30 globe artichoke   *p122*

31 ceps – wild, short, stout, stems, raised veins and tubes under cap
chanterelles – wild, funnel shaped, yellow, ribbed stalk
morels – wild, delicate beige-to-brown colour
horns of plenty – trumpet shape, shaggy, almost black
field – creamy white cap and stalk, flat cap   *p123*

32 a root: starch/sugar, little protein, some mineral salts, cellulose,
vitamins, carotene
green: rich minerals salts – calcium, iron, vitamin C, carotene
root: clean, firm, sound, even size, even shape, unblemished
green: fresh, crisp, sprouts and cabbage – compact, cauliflowers
– firm white   *p108*
b roots on racks or in bins, greens on racks, salad in a cool
place   *p110*
c roots – e.g. carrots, turnips etc., tubers – potatoes, Jerusalem
artichokes; bulbs – onions, shallots, leaves – spinach, lettuce;
brassicas – broccoli, cauliflower, pods – peas, beans, fruits –
courgette, tomatoes, stems – celery, asparagus   *p110*
d ceps – wild, short, raised veins underside
chanterelles – wild, funnel shape, yellow
morels – pale to dark, delicate   *p123*
soups, stock, sauces, salads, vegetable savouries, garnishes

Fruit

Read pp123–8 of *The Theory of Catering*.

QUESTIONS

1 Give two examples of each of the following fruit classifications
soft fruit, hard fruit, stone fruit, citrus fruit, tropical.

2 Name four English soft fruits in addition to the two in the
previous question.

3 Which are the three most used citrus fruits?

4   Are the fruits given in your previous answer available all the year round?

5   Rhubarb is in season during
      Autumn, Winter, Spring, Summer.

6   From which month do English soft fruits come into season?
      April, June, July, August.

7   Place the following in order of availability during the year of home grown
      gooseberries, cherries, damsons, currants, raspberries, plums.

8   Imported apples and pears are available all the year round: true/false.

9   Which of the following fruit are available in dried form?
      apples, gooseberries, apricots, damsons, strawberries, pears, rhubarb, figs.

10 Plums when dried are called . . . ?

11 Small grapes when dried are called . . . ?

12 Medium-sized grapes when dried are called . . . ?

13 Large grapes when dried are called . . . ?

14 Solid packed apples are apples which have been peeled, cored, quartered and
      packed tightly in cases
      frozen and packed in water in tins
      packed in water in tins
      packed in large barrels.

15 What are candied, glacé and crystallised fruits?

16 Citrus fruits are a source of vitamin . . . ?

17 Why should bananas not be stored in a refrigerator?

18 Give an example of a different fruit bought in each of the following
      a tray, a punnet, a box.

19 Give an example of each of the following
      candied fruit, crystallised item, glacé fruit.

20 From which country do we import most of our glacé, crystallised and candied fruit?
      Italy, Holland, Spain, France.

21 What kinds of fruit are the following?
   Blenheim Orange, Bramley's seedling, Comice, William,
   Avocado, Cantaloup.

22 Give the name of a chicken dish which includes banana as part of
   the garnish.

23 Name a fish dish garnished with banana.

24 Name three fruits which have both dessert and cooking varieties.

25 Name three fruits which can be used to make marmalade.

26 Bananas can be grilled, fried or eaten raw: true/false.

27 Which fruit is used to garnish fish Véronique?

28 Name three types of melon.

29 Is a honeydew melon round or oval?

30 Name four tropical fruits. Briefly describe them and give an
   example of their use.

31 Which fruit berry sauce is traditionally served with roast turkey?
   blackberry, cranberry, gooseberry, mulberry.

32 a State the grouping of fruit giving two examples of each.
     Indicate two examples of fruit commonly used in
     cooking.
   b State the food value and storage points of fruit.
   c State six ways of preserving fruits, give two examples of fruits
     preserved by each method.
   d Name and describe three types of melon. How are they assessed
     for ripeness? Describe two ways melons may be served.

ANSWERS _____

1 soft – raspberries, strawberries, redcurrants
   hard – apples, pears
   stone – plums, damsons, cherries, peaches
   citrus – oranges, lemons, limes
   tropical – dates, figs, guavas, kiwi, pineapple   *p124*

2 blackberries, bilberries, blackcurrants, loganberries   *p124*

3 oranges, lemons, grapefruit   *p124*

4 yes

5 Spring   *p125*

6 June   *p125*

7 gooseberries, raspberries, cherries, currants, plums, damsons,
       depending on variety   *p125*

8 true   *p125*

9 apples, apricots, pears, figs   *p125*

10 prunes   *p125*

11 currants   *p125*

12 sultanas   *p125*

13 raisins   *p125*

14 packed in water in tins   *p125*

15 fruits saturated in sugar   *p125*

16 C   *p124*

17 if refrigerated the skins go black   *p124*

18 tray – peaches; punnet – raspberries; box – apples   *p124*

19 candied peel, crystallised violet, glacé cherry   *p125*

20 France   *p125*

21 apple (eating), apple (cooking), pear, pear, pear, melon   *pp126–28*

22 Maryland

23 Caprice

24 apples, pears, gooseberries

25 oranges, lemons, limes   *p125*

26 true   *p127*

27 grapes   *p127*

28 ogen, honeydew, galia, cantaloup, charentais   *p128*

29 oval   *p128*

30 e.g. kiwi – small oval shape, brown, furry, fruit salad,
            pineapple – various size, oval, fruit salad, with ham, fritters
                                                                          p127

31 cranberry   *p127*

32 a i   stone – damson, peaches
              hard – apples, pears
              soft – raspberries, strawberries
              citrus – oranges, grapefruit
              tropical – bananas, pineapple
              other – cranberries, rhubarb
          ii apples, damsons, plums   *p124*
      b i   vitamin C and cellulose
          ii hard fruit in boxes, cool store
              soft fruit in punnets in cold room
              stone fruits left in containers
              bananas not in cold place   *p124*
      c freezing – blackberries, raspberries
              canning – peaches, cherries
              bottling – pears, apples
              drying (dehydration) – apricots, apples
              crystallising – apricots, cherries
              sous vide – apples, pears   *p125*
      d galia, honeydew, charentais, ogen
              slight softness when gently pressed at stalk or flower end of
              melon
              cocktail
              ½ or segment depending on type and size   *p128*

Nuts

Read pp128–30 of *The Theory of Catering*.

QUESTIONS

1   What is the food value of nuts?

2   When purchasing nuts, select those which are heavy for their size:
    true/false.

3   Name three popular dessert nuts.

4   Which nut probably has the most uses in pastry and confectionery
    work?
        almond, Brazil, walnut, pecan.

5   Give four examples of the use of nuts in pastrywork.

6   Which nut is used in desiccated form for certain curry dishes?

7   Small green nuts used for decorating are called
    filberts, adagio, cobs, pistachio

8   Name three types of nuts that are served salted.

9   a State the food value, storage and quality points of nuts.
    b Give two examples of the use of two nuts in cooking.

ANSWERS

1   mainly protein   *p128*

2   true   *p129*

3   almond, walnut, chestnut, Brazil   *p129*

4   almond   *p129*

5   gâteaux, almond paste, frangipan, congress tarts, Bakewell tart,
    decoration   *p129*

6   coconut   *p129*

7   pistachio   *p130*

8   pecan, peanuts, cashew   *p130*

9   a protein; fat and mineral salts; store in a dry, ventilated store;
      shelled nuts in air tight containers; size, weight, no mildew *p129*
    b e.g. chestnuts – stuffing, ice-cream, chestnut flour.
            coconut – curries, cakes, confectionery   *p129*

Eggs

Read pp130–4 of *The Theory of Catering*.

QUESTIONS

1   Describe the eggshell when assessing quality points for buying
    eggs.

2   When an egg is broken, describe how it should look if it is fresh.

3   Describe how the yolk should be when fresh.

4   What happens to the white of egg if it is kept too long?

5   What happens to the yolk of egg if the egg is kept too long?

6 Eggs should be stored in a
   cold very dry place; cool, dry place; cold, damp place; cool, but
   not too dry place.

7 The ideal storage place for eggs is in a refrigerator without any
   strong smelling foods at a temperature of
   0°C–5°C, 10°C–15°C, 18°C–20°C, 22°C–25°C.

8 Why should strong smelling foods not be stored near eggs?

9 Give three examples of strong smelling foods which should not be
   stored near eggs.

10 If there were a shortage of hens' eggs, which other two birds' eggs
    could be used in their place?

11 State the nutritional value of eggs.

12 Give examples of the uses of eggs
    e.g. thickening – mayonnaise
          clarifying –
          binding –
          coating –
          colouring –

13 Name the bacteria which has affected some eggs, causing food
    poisoning.

14 Which two groups of people are most likely to be affected by the
    bacteria given in your answer to the previous question?

15 What is the point of using pasteurised eggs in catering?

16 a Name four edible eggs used in the kitchen.
    b What purchasing points should be considered, how should they
       be stored, what is their food value?
    c State the seven sizes of eggs, the wholesale unit and the three
       grades.
    d Explain why the Department of Health was concerned about
       eggs.

17 a State three ways of preserving eggs.
    b Explain, with examples, why eggs are described as versatile.
    c List five of the DSS endorsements of the Code of Practice of the
       egg industry.

ANSWERS

1   clean, well shaped, strong, slightly rough   *p130*

2   high proportion of thick white to thin white   *p130*

3   firm, round, good even colour   *p130*

4   becomes thin and water passes to the yolk   *p130*

5   loss of strength, yolk flattens   *p130*

6   cool, but not too dry place   *p131*

7   0°C–5°C   *p131*

8   shells are porous, smells could be absorbed   *p131*

9   onions, fish, garlic

10   ducks, turkey, Guinea fowl   *p133*

11   most nutritients low in calories, protein easily digested, protective
     food, provide energy and help growth and repair   *p131*

12   clarifying – consommé
     binding – mixtures e.g. stuffing, minced meat
     coating – egg and crumb
     colouring – egg wash in cakes   *p133*

13   salmonella   *p132*

14   very young, old people   *p132*

15   to reduce the risk of food poisoning due to using eggs
     contaminated at source   *p132*

16   a hens, turkey, geese, ducks, quail   *p133*
     b shell – clean, well shaped, strong, rough; when broken lot of
        thick white; yolk firm, round, good colour
        in trays, blunt end up, cool – not too dry, refrigerate 0°C–5°C,
        not near smelly foods, not washed
        most nutrients – low in calories, protein, little fat   *p130*
     c 70g, 65g, 60g, 55g, 50g, 45g, under 45g
        360 eggs
        A – perfect, B – imperfect, C – for manufacturing   *p132*
     d due to outbreaks of salmonella infections   *p132*

17 **a** freezing, drying, cold storage
    b e.g.   used on all courses of menu
              clarifying – soup – consommé
              colouring – cakes, eggwash
              binding – pasta, pastes, meats
              coating – crumbing fish
              decoration – salads
              garnishing – veal viennoise
    c refrigerate eggs away from raw meat, don't use cracked egg, consume quickly, use in rotation, hand wash surfaces   *p131*

Milk

Read pp134–7 of *The Theory of Catering*.

QUESTIONS

1   Why is milk regarded as the almost perfect food?

2   Unlike eggs, milk will not absorb strong smells from other foods if kept uncovered in a refrigerator: true/false.

3   Milk is pasteurised in order to
       improve its keeping quality, improve its flavour,
       concentrate the strength, kill harmful bacteria.

4   Pasteurised milk is heated for
       15 seconds at 72°C, 20 seconds at 52°C, 25 seconds at 62°C,
       30 seconds at 72°C.

5   What is UHT milk?

6   Under sterile conditions UHT milk will keep for
       4 days, 4 weeks, 4 months, 14 months.

7   Homogenised milk has been
       pasteurised twice
       drawn from a herd of pedigree cows
       treated so that the cream is dispersed throughout the milk
       pasteurised and UHT treated.

8   Sterilised milk is produced from milk which has been
       homogenised, condensed, pasteurised, evaporated.

9   What is the ingredient in cream that causes it to be able to be whipped? B . . .

10   What is the essential difference between single and double cream?

11   What could soured cream be used for?

12   With what could clotted cream be served?

13   If cream is over-whipped it turns to
       yoghurt, cheese, margarine, butter.

14   Is there any remedy for over-whipped fresh cream? yes/no.

15   When whipping fresh cream the cream must be
       warm, cold, at blood heat, almost frozen.

16   Yoghurt is prepared from milk: true/false.

17   What is smetana?

18   What is the percentage of fat in (a) single, (b) whipping,
       (c) double cream?

19   a   How should milk be kept?
       b   Explain three of the following types of milk: pasteurised, UHT,
           homogenised, Channel Island, sterilised.
       c   Give examples of how milk is used in catering.

20   a   What is cream?
       b   What enables cream to be whipped?
       c   State three points requiring care when using cream.
       d   What is yoghurt?

ANSWERS

1	it contains all the nutrients required by the body	p134
2	false – it must always be kept covered as it easily becomes contaminated	p134
3	kill harmful bacteria	p135
4	15 seconds at 72°C	p135
5	ultra heat treated (heated to 132°C for one second)	p135
6	4 months	p135
7	treated to disperse the cream throughout the milk	p135
8	homogenised then pasteurised	p135

9 butterfat   *p136*

10 single cream minimum 18% fat, double cream 48% fat   *p138*

11 savoury dishes, salad dressing   *p138*

12 scones, fruit dishes   *p138*

13 butter   *p136*

14 no – take care not to overwhip, in hot conditions stand bowl of
cream in bowl of ice whilst whisking   *p136*

15 cold   *p136*

16 true   *p137*

17 a cross between soured cream and yoghurt   *p137*

18 single 18%, whipping 35%, double 48%   *p138*

19 **a** in delivery container, covered, refrigerated, purchased
   daily   *p136*
b e.g. pasteurised – heated 15 seconds at 72°C, cool
   rapidly   *p135*
c e.g. soups, sauces, fish, vegetables, pasta, puddings, cakes,
   sweet dishes, cold and hot drinks   *p135*

20 **a** concentrated milk fat skimmed off top of milk   *p136*
b the amount of fat it contains e.g. 35%   *p136*
c check sell by date and freshness, cold for whipping, whip in
   china or stainless steel, do not over whip, dilute before adding
   to hot foods to prevent separation   *p136*
d curd-like food   *p137*

Fats and oils

Read pp137–45 of *The Theory of Catering*.

QUESTIONS

1 Fats should be kept in a cold store or refrigerator: true/false.

2 Why should butter be kept away from strong smelling foods?

3 Why may butter be described as an energy food.

4 If kept too long butter becomes
saturated, liquid, rancid, pasteurised.

5   Why is salt added to some makes of butter in its production?

6   Butter is imported in large amounts from all but one of the following countries. Indicate the odd one out:
New Zealand, France, Denmark, Australia, Austria, Holland.

7   Butter when used for shallow frying is
homogenised, condensed, sterilised, clarified.

8   Margarine is nutritionally inferior to butter: true/false.

9   Margarine is manufactured from milk and a v. . . oil.

10   Margarine can be used in place of butter for all culinary purposes: true/false.

11   Lard is the rendered fat from
ox, pig, sheep, goat.

12   The fat content of lard is almost
100%, 90%, 80%, 70%.

13   Suet is obtained from the
kidney region of baconer pig, liver region of pork, heart region of veal, kidney region of beef.

14   Clarified animal fat is called . . .

15   Oils are fats which are liquid at room temperature: true/false.

16   Name three varieties of vegetable oil.

17   Will a good vegetable oil keep indefinitely at room temperature?

18   Which of these vegetable oils is considered to have the most flavour?
olive, groundnut, maize.

19   Name three countries from which olive oil is imported.

20   What are the best oils almost free from?

21   What is an essential requirement for an oil that is to be used for deep-frying?

22   Which of the following would you use for deep-frying?
vegetable oil, dripping, maize oil, olive oil.

23   Give the reason for your answer to the previous question.

24   Between what temperatures should frying occur?

25 **a** Name four fats and four oils. State how they should be stored.
   b What is the food value of butter and margarine?
   c Give three uses of oil and explain flash point.

ANSWERS

1	true – cold store, in warm weather in refrigerator	*p137*
2	butter can absorb strong smells	*p142*
3	because of its very high fat content	*p142*
4	rancid	*p142*
5	to act as a preservative	*p142*
6	Austria	*p142*
7	clarified	*p143*
8	false – vitamins are added	*p143*
9	vegetable oil	*p143*
10	false – e.g. not possible to produce nut brown butter or black butter for certain dishes	*p144*
11	pig	*p144*
12	100%	*p144*
13	kidney region of beef	*p144*
14	dripping	*p144*
15	true	*p144*
16	e.g. olive, soya, grape seed, walnut, sunflower, pine kernel	*p144*
17	not indefinitely, a long time in a cool place	*p144*
18	olive	*p144*
19	Spain, Greece, France, Italy	*p145*
20	flavour, odour, colour	*p145*
21	low flash point	*p145*
22	all could be used but vegetable and maize oils suitable	*p145*
23	olive oil would be very expensive, dripping has flavour and could be greasy	*p145*

24 between 75°C and 180°C   *p145*

25 **a** butter, margarine, lard, dripping
          sunflower, maize, ground nut, grape seed, olive, palm
          fats: cold store/refrigerate, oils: cool place   *pp137–45*
       b energy food due to fat content, margarine not inferior to butter
          nutritionally   *pp142–43*
       c vinaigrette, mayonnaise, shallow frying, deep frying, to exclude
          air
          flash point: the temperature when heated oil is likely to ignite
                                                                 pp144–45

Cheese

Read pp146–9 of *The Theory of Catering.*

QUESTIONS

1   What is cheese made from?

2   List the four main types of cheese and give an example of each.

3   Which cheese is made from goat's milk?
          Parmesan, Edam, Chèvre, Brie.

4   Which cheese is made from ewe's milk?
          Gorgonzola, Roquefort, Stilton, Danish blue.

5   Where should cheese be stored?

6   Why is cheese a nutritious food?

7   The skin or rind of cheese should not show spots of m . . . as this
         is a sign of damp storage.

8   When cut, cheese should not give off an over-strong s . . . or any
         indication of a . . .

9   Name three hard, three soft and three blue vein cheeses.

10   Hard, semi-hard and blue vein cheese when cut should not
         appear . . .

11   Soft cheese when cut should not appear r . . . but should have a
         delicate c . . . consistency.

12   The chief fermenting agent used in cheese making is
          junket, plunket, rennet, sonnet.

13 Name four English varieties of cheese.

14 Delete the odd one out in each line
    Cheddar, Cheshire, Camembert, Gruyère, Parmesan.
    Stilton, Bel Paese, Roquefort, Danish blue.

15 Name one cheese from each of the following countries
    France, Italy, Holland, Switzerland, Denmark, England.

16 The hardest cheese which is produced for grating is
    Port Salut, Pommel demi-Swiss, Parmesan, Bel Paese.

17 Which cheese is known as the King of Cheeses?

18 Name two cheeses from Scotland.

19 Name one Welsh cheese.

20 Which cheeses fit the correct description:

a	White, soft, crumbly, clean, mild flavour.	Double Gloucester
b	Orange-red, buttery, open texture, delicate creamy flavour.	Cheddar
c	White with blue veins, soft, close texture, strong flavour.	Lancashire
d	Golden colour, close texture, clean, mellow, nutty flavour.	Stilton

21 Arrange the following cheeses to fit the countries of origin.

Caboc	Greece
Roquefort	Switzerland
Ricotta	Holland
Cambazola	Italy
Edam	Germany
Gruyère	France
Fetta	Scotland

22 What do the following cheeses have in common?
    Gorgonzola, Roquefort, Cambazola, Stilton.

23 What do the following cheeses have in common?
    quark, fromage frais, curd cheese, cottage cheese.

24 What are
    a fromage frais
    b quark?

25 What points should be considered regarding a cheeseboard?

26 Name one soup dish, one egg dish, one fish dish, one vegetable dish and one savoury dish, where cheese is used.

27 a Name three sources of cheese and state how quality is recognised.
    b Briefly explain the process of producing cheese.
    c State the food value of cheese and explain how cheese should be stored.
    d Give five varied uses of cheese.

ANSWERS

1	Cow's, ewe's or goat's milk	*p146*
2	e.g. hard – Parmesan, semi-hard – Edam, blue-vein – Stilton, soft – Brie.	*p146*
3	Chèvre	*p148*
4	Roquefort	*p148*
5	cool, dry, well-ventilated store	*p147*
6	concentrated food containing all the nutrients	*p147*
7	mildew	*p146*
8	smell, ammonia	*p146*
9	hard – Gruyère, Cheddar, Edam soft – Brie, Camembert, Ricotta blue vein – Danish blue, Gorgonzola, Roquefort	*pp146–49*
10	dry	*p146*
11	runny, creamy	*p146*
12	rennet	*p146*
13	Cheddar, Gloucester, Cheshire, Stilton, Lancashire, Leicester, Wensleydale, Derby	*p148*
14	Parmesan – only used for cooking or garnish Bel paese – not a blue vein cheese	*pp148–49*
15	French – Port Salut, Italian – Mozzarella, Dutch – Edam, Swiss – Gruyère, Danish – Blue vein, English – Cheddar	*p149*

16 Parmesan   *p147*

17 Stilton   *p148*

18 Dunlop, Caboc   *p148*

19 Caerphilly   *p148*

20 **a** Lancashire   **c** Stilton
        b Double Gloucester   **d** Cheddar   *p148*

21 Cabac – Scotland, Roquefort – France, Ricotta – Italy, Edam –
        Holland, Gruyère – Switzerland, Fetta – Greece   *pp148–49*

22 all blue vein   *pp148–49*

23 all soft cheeses   *p149*

24 **a** fat free, soft curd, cheese
        b salt, fat free, soft cheese made from skimmed milk   *p149*

25 good selection – variety of texture, colour, taste, appearance, prime
        condition   *p147*

26 e.g. soup – minestrone, egg – cheese omelette, pasta, macaroni
        gratin, fish – scallops mornay, vegetable – cauliflower cheese;
        savoury – Welsh rarebit   *p147*

27 **a** cow's, ewe's, goat's
          mildew, dryness, smell, not runny   *p146*
        b acidity test, soured with starter, rennet added, stirred, warmed,
          settled, liquid run off (whey), remainder (curds) ground, salted,
          moulded, stored   *p146*
        c fat, protein, mineral salts, vitamins
          store cool, dry, well ventilated, turn whole cheeses, store on its
          own   *p147*
        d e.g. cheese board, omelette, Mornay sauce, minestrone,
          cauliflower cheese, sole florentine, Welsh rarebit.   *p147*

Cereals

Read pp149–61 of *The Theory of Catering*.

QUESTIONS

1 All the following cereals are used in catering: true/false
        wheat, oats, barley, maize, rice, tapioca, sago, arrowroot.

2   All cereals contain large amounts of . . .

3   What is flour produced from?

4   Which of the following vitamins do whole grain cereals provide:
     A, B, C.

5   In what atmosphere should flour be stored?

6   What is the difference between strong and soft flour?

7   Name three foods for which soft flour is suitable.

8   Name three foods for which strong flour is suitable.

9   What percentage of the whole grain is contained in
     wholemeal flour, wheatmeal flour, white flour?

10   What is added to white flour to make it self raising?

11   What is semolina?

12   Which is the odd one out and why?
     vermicelli, spaghetti, macaroni, minestrone.

13   Oats have the highest food value of all the cereals: true/false.

14   State four ways of using oats.

15   From which cereal is cornflour obtained?
     wheat, oats, maize, barley.

16   Maize, sweetcorn, corn, corn on the cob are different names for
     the same food: true/false.

17   When cooked, long grain rice has a . . . structure.

18   When cooked, short grain rice has a . . . structure.

19   What is obtained from
     a the roots of the cassava plant?
     b the pith of a certain palm?
     c the roots of the West Indian maranta plant?

20   Why is arrowroot particulary suitable for thickening clear sauces?

21   Arrowroot is suitable for invalids because it is easily digested:
     true/false.

22   a Define cereals, name four used in the kitchen.
     b State the food value and storage of cereals.
     c Briefly explain the production of flour and describe three types
       of flour.

d Where is rice grown? Define the three main types, giving an example of the use of each.

ANSWERS

1	true	*p150*
2	starch	*p149*
3	cereal grains which are ground	*p150*
4	vitamin B	*p150*
5	dry, well ventilated	*p150*
6	the percentage of gluten proteins – soft flour contains less than strong flour	*p150*
7	cake, biscuits, soups, sauces	*p151*
8	bread, puff paste, Italian pasta	*p151*
9	wholemeal 100%, wheatmeal 85–95%, white 72–85%	*p150*
10	cream of tartar and bicarbonate of soda	*p150*
11	granulated hard flour from central part of wheat grain	*p150*
12	minestrone is a soup, the others are pastas	
13	true	*p151*
14	e.g. porridge, oatcakes, haggis, thickening soup, coating fish	*p151*
15	maize	*p152*
16	true	*p152*
17	firm	*p152*
18	soft	*p152*
19	cassava – tapioca, palm – sago, maranta – arrowroot	*p161*
20	it becomes transparent when boiled	*p161*
21	true	*p161*
22	**a** cultivated grasses – wheat, oats, rye, barley, maize, rice	*p149*
	b energy food – whole grain vitamin B dry store, well ventilated, in containers with lids.	*p150*

c grains broken, parts separated, sifted, blended, ground
white flour – 75% whole endosperm
wholemeal – 100% whole grain
wheatmeal – 90% whole grain
Hovis – 85% whole grain
self-raising – cream of tartar and bi-carbonated soda added *p150*
d Far East, South America, Italy, USA
long – savoury, plain boiled
medium – all purpose e.g. risotto
short – milk puddings   *p152*

Raising agents

Read pp161–3 of *The Theory of Catering*.

QUESTIONS

1   Name three food processes in which air is used as a raising agent.

2   Baking powder is a chemical raising agent: true/false.

3   List five hints on using baking powder.

4   What is yeast?
    a fungus form of plant life
    a chemically produced raising agent
    concentrated hops
    double strength baking powder.

5   State four essential storage and quality points for fresh yeast.

6   Yeast should always be used at room temperature: true/false.

7   Yeast contains vitamin B: true/false.

8   To enable yeast to grow which conditions are necessary?
    moisture, heat, salt
    cold liquid, sugar, proving
    hot liquid, salt, sugar
    blood heat, liquid, sugar, proving.

9   Does salt retard the working of yeast?

10 Above which temperature is yeast destroyed?
    12°C, 22°C, 42°C, 52°C.

11 What effect does salt have on yeast?

12 Why should yeast dough be well kneaded?

13 Give another word meaning *kneading*.

14 *Proving* a yeast dough means
    letting it rest, cutting it back, allowing it to double in size, it has
    satisfied the customers.

15 Name six items that are made using yeast.

16 What causes over-proving?

17 **a** State four ways foods may be aerated, giving an example of
    each.
    b List four points to consider when using baking powder.
    c How should yeast be purchased and stored?
    d State five points to remember when using yeast. Explain
    kneading and proving.

ANSWERS _____

1   sifting, rubbing in, whisking, layering   *p161*

2   true   *p162*

3   mix in thoroughly, use fresh, measure accurately, keep lid on tin,
    do not slam oven doors   *p162*

4   fungus form of plant life   *p162*

5   store in cold place, keep wrapped, use fresh and moist, should
    crumble easily, ordered as required, be pale grey in colour, have a
    pleasing smell   *p162*

6   true   *p163*

7   true   *p162*

8   blood heat, liquid, sugar, proving   *p163*

9   yes   *p163*

10 over 52°C   *p163*

11 regards the action of yeast, the more salt the slower the
    action   *p163*

12 to distribute yeast evenly   *p163*

13 working   *p163*

14 allowing it to double in size   *p163*

15 e.g. bread, rolls, buns, croissants, Danish pastry, baba, frying
batter   *p163*

16 excess and uneven heat and too long a proving time   *p163*

17 **a** whisking – meringues
baking powder – steamed pudding
yeast – bread
lamination – puff paste   *p161*
b mix, measure, use within month, lids firm, oven doors   *p162*
c wrap, order as required, pleasant smell, pale grey, cool place,
crumble, moist   *p162*
d salt retards, use room temperature, avoid draughts, best
temperature 21°C–27°C, liquid temperature 36°C–37°C,
destroyed over 52°C, warm flour and bowl
kneading: worked to make elastic, to distribute yeast, elasticity
allows gases to expand
proving: allow dough to double in size, warm, draught free
place, knock back – press down to original size and allow to
prove again; prove after moulding and before baking; allows
yeast to come into contact with dough again and improves
distribution of yeast   *p163*

Sugar

Read pp163–4 of *The Theory of Catering*.

QUESTIONS

1   Sugar is invaluable for producing energy: true/false.

2   Name the two main sources of sugar.

3   What percentage of pure sugar is contained in sugar?
100%, 80%, 60%, 40%.

4   Demerara sugar is
brown sugar, lump sugar, coffee sugar, fine caster sugar.

5   Brown sugar is unrefined: true/false.

6   List the following in order of fineness with the finest first
icing sugar, granulated sugar, caster sugar.

7   What is loaf sugar?

8 Give an example of the use of each of these
glucose, syrup, treacle.

9 **a** i State the two sources of sugar.
ii Specify its food value.
iii Give examples of the three types of sugar.
b i Explain briefly the production of sugar.
ii Name two items produced during the process other than sugar.
c State four varied uses of sugar.

ANSWERS

1 true   *p163*

2 beet and cane   *p163*

3 almost 100%   *p163*

4 brown sugar   *p163*

5 true – unrefined   *p163*

6 icing, caster, granulated   *p164*

7 cake sugar produced by pressing crystals when wet then drying and cutting into blocks   *p164*

8 glucose – confectionery e.g. fondant
syrup – steamed pudding
treacle – tarts   *p164*

9 **a** i beet, cane
ii energy food
iii refined – granulated, caster
unrefined – brown sugar
partially refined – Demerara, light brown   *p163*
b i extracted – crystallised, refined, sieved
ii syrup and treacle   *p163*
c e.g. sweetening – pastry and confectionery
colouring – caramel
decoration – spun sugar
beverages – tea, coffee
sauces – mint   *p164*

Beverages

Read pp164–75 of *The Theory of Catering*.

QUESTIONS

1   Into what two categories may drink be classified?

2   Give six categories of alcoholic drinks.

3   State six non-alcoholic drinks.

4   What are the two types of mineral water available?

5   Name
         two aromatised wines, two fortified wines, two liqueurs.

6   What is the main ingredient other than water used to produce
     a cider
     b perry.

7   Is it correct that non-carbonated waters are sparkling?

8   State four factors which affect the quality and characteristics of wine.

9   Besides red and white wine, what is the third grouping?

10   Match the following.

Stilton	raspberry liqueur
trifle	port
fish sauce	rum
carbonnade of beef	Madeira
tripe	dry white wine
sorbet	beer
baba	sherry
ox tongue	cider

11   **a** Both coffee and cocoa are used as a drink. Explain three culinary
         uses of coffee and three of cocoa, other than as beverages.
     b Milk is a versatile commodity. Explain how it may be used in
         beverages and in four different dishes for four courses on the
         menu.
     c Name different dishes using
             Madeira, a liqueur, mineral water, beer, red wine.

12   **a** With which alcoholic drink is Stilton associated?
     b Which kind of white wine is usually used with shallow poached
         fish?

c Name a soup to which an alcoholic liquid may be added.

d State three uses of alcoholic drink in pastry.

ANSWERS

1	alcoholic and non-alcoholic	*p165*
2	wines, beers, spirits, ciders, fortified wine, liqueurs etc.	*p165*
3	water, tea, coffee, cocoa, milk, mineral water, fruit juices etc.	*p165*
4	sparkling and still	*p165*

5   a Vermouth, Dubonnet, Campari
     b Sherry, Port, Madeira.
     c Cointreau, Cherry Brandy, Grand Marnier etc.   *p173*

6   a cider – apples
     b perry – pears   *p175*

7   incorrect, they are still

8   grape variety, climate, soil, production method   *p172*

9   rosé   *p173*

10 Stilton – port
     trifle – sherry
     fish sauce – dry white wine
     carbonnade of beef – beer
     tripe – cider
     sorbet – raspberry liqueur
     baba – rum
     ox tongue – Madeira

11 a coffee – e.g. gâteaux, ice cream, éclairs, bavarois, mousse   *p165*
     cocoa – e.g. gâteaux, ice cream, chocolate sauce, chocolate
     pudding, soufflé, mousse   *p171*
    b milk – in tea, coffee, cocoa, on its own, milk shakes, chocolate
     drink   *p172*
     e.g.   soups – cream soups
           fish – parsley sauce, poached in milk
           poultry – cream sauces, chicken cutlets, pancakes
           vegetables – cream or béchamel sauce with e.g. carrots,
           cauliflower, potato purée
           sweets – milk puddings, bavarois, custard sauce, pastry
           cream, pancakes
           pasta – macaroni cheese, gnocchi

   c Madeira – e.g. braised ox tongue
     beer – carbonnade of beef
     liqueur – soufflé Grand Marnier
     red wine – Coq au vin
     mineral water – Vichy carrots

12 a port
   b dry
   c consommé
   d sorbets, soufflés, sauces

Coffee

Read pp165–9 of *The Theory of Catering*.

QUESTIONS

1 Name four varieties of coffee.

2 What is the correct way to store coffee?

3 Which coffee is less of a stimulant? Explain why.

4 List six points to follow when making coffee.

5 How much coffee is required to produce 1 litre?

6 a What is coffee? Name four places exporting coffee.
   b State the three ways it may be purchased and the purchasing unit.
   c Give six methods of making coffee. Describe two methods.
   d Other than as a beverage, give three examples of the use of coffee.

ANSWERS

1 Mysore, Java, Brazil, Kenya — *p165*

2 airtight containers in well ventilated dry store — *p166*

3 decaffeinated because the caffeine has been removed — *p165*

4 use good quality coffee beans, freshly roasted and ground, fresh water, freshly boiled, measure carefully, strain, use within 30 minutes — *p166*

5 60–65g — *p166*

6   **a** bean of coffee tree
          Brazil, Columbia, Kenya, Indonesia   *p165*
     b unroasted, roasted, ground
          7lb and 28lb   *p165*
     c jug, percolator, still set, filter, plunger pot, Cona, Espresso,
          Turkish
          e.g. jug – boiling water poured onto coffee grounds
          stand for few minutes, strained   *p166*
     d cakes, icing, sweets, ice cream   *p165*

Tea

Read pp169–70 of *The Theory of Catering*.

QUESTIONS

1   Name five tea producing countries.

2   Tea without sugar and/or milk has no nutritional value:
     true/false.

3   Why must tea be kept in airtight containers?

4   State four golden rules for making good tea.

5   **a** What is tea?
     b How is it purchased and stored?

ANSWERS

1   India, China, Sri Lanka, Pakistan, Indonesia, Uganda, Kenya,
     Tanzania, Malawi   *p169*
2   true   *p170*

3   To prevent it becoming moist, also prevents tea absorbing
     smells.   *p170*

4   Good quality tea, fresh water, freshly boiled, time to brew   *p170*

5   **a** dried leaves of tea plants   *p169*
     b packs from ½g to 100lb; individual tea bags to tea chests
          dry, clean, airtight containers, well ventilated store. *p170*

Cocoa

Read pp170–1 of *The Theory of Catering*.

QUESTIONS

1   Cocoa is a powder produced from the beans of the cacao tree: true/false.

2   Does cocoa have any food value?

3   Chocolate is produced from cocoa mass, fine sugar and cocoa butter: true/false.

4   Give three uses of chocolate couverture.

5   **a** What is cocoa, from where is it imported and how is it stored?
    b State two main uses, giving examples.

ANSWERS

1   true   *p170*

2   some protein and starch and some iron   *p171*

3   true   *p171*

4   icing, butter cream, sauces, dipping chocolates, shapes   *p171*

5   **a** powder produced from cocoa bean from West Africa, stored in
        air tight containers, ventilated store
    b as a beverage – cocoa, drinking chocolate
        producing chocolate – petit fours, gâteaux
        flavour – puddings, sauces, ice cream, cakes   *p171*

Pulses

Read pp175–6 of *The Theory of Catering*.

QUESTIONS

1   Pulses are dried s . . . of plants which form p . . .

2   Pulses are a good source of protein: true/false.

3   How would you describe the following
        flageolets, haricot, dahl.

4   Which pulse items fit the following descriptions?
     Pink splotched mottled colour.
     Resembles the kernel of a small hazel nut.
     Small, brown, knobbly.

5   What could these beans be used for?
     mung beans, soya beans, red kidney beans.

6   **a** Define pulses.
     b What is their food value?
     c How should they be stored?
     d State how they can be used and give four varied menu examples.

ANSWERS

1   pulses are the dried seeds of plants which form pods.   *p175*

2   true – very good source   *p175*

3   flageolet – pale green kidney shaped bean
     haricot – white smooth oval bean
     dahl – Hindi word for dried peas and beans   *p176*

4   borlotti, chick-pea, ful medames   *p176*

5   mung – bean sprouts
     soya – sauce
     red kidney – chilli con carne   *p176*

6   **a** dried seeds of leguminous plants which form pods
        seeds are dried and kept in a dry condition
     b good source of protein and carbohydrate
        very useful in vegetarian diets
     c clean containers in dry ventilated store
     d soups; stews; vegetables; salads; vegetarian dishes
        e.g. three bean salad; green pea soup; haricot oxtail; lentil and
        courgette flan   *p176*

Herbs

Read pp176–9 of *The Theory of Catering*.

QUESTIONS

1   What value have herbs from the nutritional point of view?
     To provide body regulating processes.

> Enable starch to be converted to sugar.
> Create energy from carbohydrate.
> Stimulate the flow of gastric juices.

2   Name five common herbs and state a suitable use for each.

3   Herbs may be used f . . . but the majority are d . . .

4   What is it in the leaves of herbs that gives the characteristic smell and flavour?
> pollen, flower buds, oil, the stems.

5   Which herb is a member of the onion family and has a delicate onion flavour?

6   Which is the strong pungent herb that aids the stomach to digest rich fatty meat such as pork, duck, goose?

7   What is the composition of fines-herbes?

ANSWERS

1	stimulate the flow of gastric juices	p176
2	e.g. mint – sauce	
	sage – stuffing	
	fennel– fish dishes	
	bay – sauces, stews	
	parsley – garnishing, sauces	p177
3	fresh – dried	p176
4	oil	p176
5	chives	p177
6	sage	p178
7	parsley, chervil, tarragon	p179

Spices

Read pp179–83 of *The Theory of Catering*.

QUESTIONS

1   Spices are a variety of fruits, seeds, roots, flowers or bark of different trees or shrubs: true/false.

2   Allspice is another name for mixed spice: true/false.

3   Cloves are
     unopened flower buds of a tree from Zanzibar
     the fruit of a shrub from Penang
     the flower buds of a shrub from Morocco
     unopened flower buds of a tree from Madagascar.

4   Which spice is associated with the cooking of apples?

5   What are caraway seeds used for?

6   Which tropical tree bears a fruit like an apricot which when ripe
     has a kernel which is . . . The kernel is covered with a bright red
     covering which is . . .

7   Name four spices which go into mixed spice.

8   State a different use for each of these
     nutmeg, saffron, ginger.

9   Saffron is the dried stigmas from a crocus grown chiefly in
     Spain, Portugal, Italy.

10   Which of these items are used with fish dishes?
     dill seeds, anise, fennel seeds.

11   What are the following?
     fenugreek, garam masala, cardamom, Chinese five spice powder.

12   a What are herbs and what is their value?
     b Name two and give an example of the use of each.
     c What are spices and where are they grown?

ANSWERS

1   true   *p179*

2   false – it is the unripe fruit of West Indian pimemto tree which is
     dried and ground.   *p179*

3   unopened flower buds of a tree from Zanzibar.   *p181*

4   cloves   *p181*

5   seed cake, certain bread and cheeses   *p180*

6   nutmeg, mace   *p182*

7   allspice, coriander, cloves, nutmeg, cinnamon, ginger   *p183*

8   nutmeg – milk puddings
     saffron – savoury rice
     ginger – pudding, curry   *p182*

9   Spain   *p182*

10   all   *p180*

11   fenugreek – ground and used in curry
     garam masala – a mixture of hot spices
     cardamom – used in curry
     Chinese five spice – mixture of anise powder, fennel, clove,
     cinnamon, anise pepper   *pp181–82*

12   a herbs – leaves of plants which are used fresh or dried which
        stimulate the gastric juices   *pp176–77*
     b e.g.   mint – mint sauce
               thyme – stuffings   *pp176–77*
     c spices are dried fruits, seeds, root or bark of certain trees or
        shrubs mainly from Asia, West Indies, Africa.   *p179*

Condiments

Read pp183–5 of *The Theory of Catering*.

QUESTIONS

1   What causes the differences between white and black peppercorns?

2   Why is salt necessary in the diet?

3   What happens to salt if it is not kept dry?

4   From what is pepper obtained?

5   Which is the hotter – cayenne or paprika?

6   Paprika is a
         type of herb, oriental spice, mild pepper, kind of mustard.

7   Paprika is used in a specific dish known as . . .

8   From which country did the dish named in the previous question
     originate?

9   In which part of Great Britain is mustard grown?
         East Anglia, Scilly Isles, East Lanarkshire, Lancashire.

10 Malt vinegar is made from oats: true/false.

11 Name three types of vinegar.

12 Name the most expensive vinegar which has the most delicate flavour.

13 State two uses of vinegar other than preservation.

14 **a** How should salt be stored, for what is it used, how is it obtained?

    b How is pepper obtained? Give examples of its use. Name three kinds of pepper.

    c Give two examples of mustard and examples of the use of each.

ANSWERS

1	white pepper is produced from black pepper which has had the skin removed	*p184*
2	for stabilising body fluids and preventing cramp	*p183*
3	grains adhere together, it does not flow or sprinkle	*p183*
4	a tropical shrub	*p183*
5	cayenne	*p184*
6	mild pepper	*p184*
7	goulash	*p184*
8	Hungary	*p184*
9	East Anglia	*p184*
10	false – barley is used	*p184*
11	malt, spirit, artificial	*p184*
12	grape based	*p184*
13	salad dressing, as a reduction, flavouring	*p184*

14 **a** salt must be kept dry
    at the table, preserving, seasoning dishes
    obtained from mines or sea

    b black and white pepper
    grinding peppercorns, chillies or capsicums
    cayenne, paprika

    c English – at table, Welsh rarebit
    Continental – at table, vinaigrette   *pp183–85*

Colourings, flavourings and essences

Read pp185–6 of *The Theory of Catering*.

QUESTIONS

1   What colour is cochineal?
2   Match the colours to their culinary sources
        green   tumeric
        red   chlorophyll
        brown   cochineal
        yellow   blackjack

3   What could anchovy essence be used for?

ANSWERS

1   red   *p185*

2   green – chlorophyll   brown – blackjack (sugar)
    red – cochineal   yellow – tumeric, saffron, egg yolks   *p185*

3   fish sauces, fish dishes   *p186*

Grocery, delicatessen and confectionery goods

Read pp186–96 of *The Theory of Catering*.

QUESTIONS

1   What is *aspic* jelly?

2   *Bombay duck* is
        a small Indian duck, an eastern type of sweet, dried fillet of fish,
        a Chinese hors-d'oeuvre.

3   Caviar is obtained from
        cod, carp, salmon, sturgeon.

4   The finest caviar comes from
        France, Italy, or Spain
        Russian, Iran (Persia), or Romania
        Hungary, Yugoslavia, or Arabia
        Holland, Belgium, or Denmark.

5   *Cèpes* are a
     species of French mushroom, kind of Italian pasta, type of
     French pancake, variety of Italian pear.

6   What is *foie gras*?

7   *Galantine* is a
     cooked meat preparation, type of salami, kind of haggis, special
     vegetable dish.

8   Name the two forms in which gelatine is available and give an
     example of its use.

9   What are *gherkins*?

10   Name the three main varieties of olive.

11   With which countries are the following associated?
     frog's legs, haggis, Parma ham, foie gras, olives, sauerkraut,
     poppadum, Stilton, truffles, escargots.

12   Give an example of the use of
     capers, gherkins, olives.

13   Are walnuts pickled before or after the shell has hardened?

14   *Poppadums* are
     poppy seeds, Indian breakfast cereal, an exotic oriental fruit,
     thin round biscuits.

15   Potted shrimps are preserved in
     margarine, oil, vegetable oil, butter.

16   *Rollmops* are
     curled anchovies, dainty bread rolls, rolled herring fillets, rolled
     kipper fillets.

17   Sauerkraut is made from
     white cabbage, green cabbage, red cabbage, a mixture of all
     three.

18   The ideal weight of a salmon for smoking is
     2½–5kilos, 6–8kilos, 10–11½kilos, 12½–15kilos.

19   At which course would smoked salmon usually be served?

20   What are *escargots*?

21   How would escargots be served?

22 What are truffles? Name the famous area in France where they are found.

23 A *marron glacé* is a peeled and cooked chestnut preserved in syrup: true/false.

24 What is honey?

25 *Pastillage* is a mixture of what two ingredients?

26 Rennet is used for making
   aspic, jelly, junket, fondant.

27 a Give three examples of using colouring and two examples of using essences in catering.
   b Select from caviar, foie gras or truffles. Give a description of the one selected.
   c Name three pickled items. State their use in the kitchen.

28 Explain how it is possible to keep abreast of food prices.

ANSWERS

1   clear savoury jelly; may be made with fresh ingredients or in dried
       form   *p187*

2   dried fillet of fish   *p187*

3   sturgeon   *p187*

4   Russia, Iran (Persia), Romania   *p187*

5   mushroom   *p187*

6   goose liver delicacy   *p188*

7   cooked meat preparation   *p189*

8   leaf, powdered, aspic, bavarois   *p189*

9   pickled small cucumber   *p190*

10 Manzanilla, Spanish queens, black   *p190*

11 France, Scotland, Italy, France, Greece, Germany, India, England,
       France, France   *pp187–91*

12 capers – caper sauce, piquant sauce
       gherkins – garnish, tartare sauce
       olives – hors-d'oeuvre, cocktail savouries   *p190*

13 before   *p190*

14 thin round biscuits   *p190*

15 butter   *p190*

16 rolled herring fillets   *p190*

17 white cabbage   *p190*

18 6–8kilos   *p189*

19 first course   *p189*

20 snails   *p191*

21 in a special dish in their shells in garlic butter   *p191*

22 fungi, Périgord   *p191*

23 true   *p193*

24 a natural sugar produced by bees working on the nectar of flowers
                                                                         p192

25 gum tragacanth and icing sugar (gelatine may also be used in place
    of gum tragacanth)   *p193*

26 junket   *p196*

27 **a** cochineal – gâteaux with pink icing
       yellow – saffron in rice
       brown – brown sauces, gravies
       coffee – coffee éclairs
       vanilla – caramel cream, almond cakes   *p185*

    b e.g. caviar, define preparation, types, sources, cost, storage,
       service   *pp187–91*

    c e.g. gherkins – tartare sauce, garnish, decoration
       mango chutney – accompaniment for curry
       walnuts – canapé Ivanhoe
       capers – sauce, skate with black butter   *p190*

28 visit markets, shops, supermarkets, etc., price lists from retailer,
    wholesaler, *Caterer and Hotelkeeper* magazine.

ELEMENTARY NUTRITION, FOOD SCIENCE AND FOOD PRESERVATION

Read pp196–232 of *The Theory of Catering*.

Elementary nutrition

QUESTIONS

1   Give a brief definition of food.

2   List the six nutrients.

3   What is the study of nutrients known as?

4   Which food contains only one nutrient?
      egg, apple, sugar, flour.

5   For the body to obtain maximum benefit from food it is essential
      that everyone concerned with buying, storage, cooking and serving
      of food and the compiling of menus should have some knowledge
      of what?

6   What is digestion?

7   What assists food digestion?

8   To enable the body to benefit from food it must be absorbed into
      the blood stream: true/false.

9   When does absorption take place?
      when drinking with food, at the same time as digestion, after
      the food has been broken down, just before digestion.

10   Describe food so that the body fully benefits from it.

11   What do you understand by a *state of malnutrition*?

12   Rearrange the following tables of the main functions of nutrients
      correctly.

Energy	Growth and repair	Regulation of body processes
Proteins	Water	Minerals
Fats	Carbohydrates	Proteins
Vitamins	Minerals	Water

13 Name the two kinds of protein.

14 Why does the body need protein?

15 Do growing children and expectant mothers need more protein than other adults?

16 Explain the reason for your answer to the previous question.

17 List four foods that give the main supply of protein in the average diet.

18 Protein is composed of . . . acids.

19 All these acids are essential to the body: true/false.

20 The protein of cheese is different from the protein of meat because the arrangement of the . . . is not the same.

21 Which is the odd one out and why?
     onion, herring, lamb chop, split pea soup, cornflakes.

22 Moderately cooked protein is digested most easily: true/false.

23 Give an example to illustrate your answer to the previous question.

24 What are the two main groups of fats?

25 State three functions of fats.

26 Indicate the origin of the following foods by writing A for animal and V for vegetable.
     butter, cod liver oil, margarine, sunflower oil, soya bean, suet, nuts, bacon, olive oil, meat fat, lard, halibut liver oil, herring, cream, dripping, cheese.

27 Olive oil is a fat which is liquid at room temperature: true/false.

28 Which is the odd one out and why?
     herring, walnuts, olives, bacon, blackcurrants, avocado pear.

29 Fats differ because of the . . . acids from which they are derived.

30 Give three examples of fatty acids.

31 What two things do fatty acids affect?

32 Fats provide the body with . . . and . . .

33 List six oily fish.

34 Name the three main groups of carbohydrates.

The function of carbohydrates is to provide the body with most of its

vitamins, protection, carbon, energy.

36 Name three foods which are main suppliers of carbohydrate in the diet.

37 Sugar is the simplest form of carbohydrate: true/false.

38 Match the following

maltose	beet and cane sugar
lactose	fruit
sucrose	milk
glucose	honey and animal blood
fructose	grain

39 Which of the following foods contribute starch to the diet?
rice, beef, flour, plaice, peas, butter beans, onions, apples.

40 Give three examples of foods containing starch in each of the following categories
whole grains, powdered grains, vegetables, unripe fruit, cereals, cooked starch, pasta.

41 Cellulose is the
skin of fresh fish
sinew of meat
coarser structure of vegetables and cereals
most complex of all the vitamins.

42 What is the purpose of cellulose in the diet?

43 What is roughage also known as?

44 Vitamins are the chemical substances which are . . . for life.

45 Vitamins are produced both naturally and synthetically: true/false.

46 Give two examples of the general functions of vitamins.

47 In which of the following is Vitamin A found?
liver, lamb, butter, cooking fat, herrings, plaice, carrots, apricots, cheese, cauliflower, milk, cherries.

48 Vitamin A is fat soluble: true/false.

49 List three functions of vitamins.

50 Which vitamin is necessary for healthy bones and teeth?

51 Which two vitamins are added to margarine?

52 Name the most important source of vitamin D.

53 Name three groups of foods containing vitamin D.

54 Is vitamin B required to enable the body to obtain energy from the carbohydrates?

55 Name three foods in which vitamin B is found.

56 List the three main substances which make up vitamin B group.

57 Can vitamin B be lost in cooking?

58 Which of the following foods are sources of B1 Thiamin, Riboflavin or Niacin?
wholemeal bread, cheese, kidney, bacon, liver, peas, yeast, meat extract, brewers' yeast, oatmeal, beef, eggs.

59 What is another name for *Niacin*?

60 Vitamin C can be lost in cooking and by bad s . . .

61 Name six foods containing vitamin C.

62 Match the following
egg yolk   vitamin A
kidney   vitamin B
oranges   vitamin C
yeast   vitamin D

63 Which three of the following mineral elements are most likely to be deficient in the diet?
calcium, sodium, phosphorus, potassium, iron, iodine.

64 List the three sources of each of the mineral elements selected in the previous question.

65 The use that the body makes of calcium is dependent on the presence of vitamin . . .

66 Name two foods that are sources of calcium.

67 What is the mineral element needed particularly for growing bones and teeth and for expectant and nursing mothers?

68 The body makes use of phosphorus in conjunction with c . . . and vitamin . . .

69 Which four of the following foods are sources of phosphorus?
liver, cheese, eggs, lettuce, fish, spinach.

70   Iron is required for building the haemoglobin in blood and is therefore necessary for transporting . . . and . . . . . . round the body.

71   Which three of the following foods are sources of iron?
       lean meat, tomatoes, offal, carrots, egg yolk, cream.

72   Which mineral element is found in all body fluids and is found in salt?

73   Which mineral element do we lose from the body when we perspire?

74   Water is required for which body functions?
       M . . . , A . . . , D . . . , B . . . , E . . . , S . . .

75   Excluding liquids, name six foods that contain water.

76   Match the following

protein	nutritive value not affected by normal cooking
carbohydrate	lost by cooking and keeping hot
fat	destroyed by high temperature and use of bicarbonate soda
iron	may be acquired from pans in which food is cooked
vitamin B1	needs to be thoroughly cooked
vitamin C	overcooking reduces nutritive value

77   Does overcooking have an effect on the nutritive value of food?

78   Unless starch is thoroughly cooked it cannot be properly digested: true/false.

79   Is the nutritive value of fat affected by cooking?

80   Which of the following vitamins can withstand cooking temperatures and are not lost in cooking?
       A, B, C, D.

81   Why is energy required by the body?

82   a Foods containing a high fat content will have a high . . .
       b Foods containing a lot of water will have a low . . .

83   By which term is the energy value of food measured?
       calcium, calcius, celanus, calorie.

84 People engaged in energetic work require more calories than people engaged in sedentary occupations: true/false.

85 Who needs the highest daily calorie intake?
A young male apprentice aged 19 playing football two evenings a week.
A young lady receptionist who attends a disco once a week.
An office typist who is a keen television fan.
An accountant who is studying hard for examinations.

86 What is often said to be the almost perfect food?

87 Why is margarine sometimes more nutritious than butter?

88 Why is the food value of cheese exceptional?

89 What does bacon contain nutritionally that is not present in other meats?

90 Cheaper cuts of meat are less nourishing than more expensive cuts of meat: true/false.

91 When bones of tinned salmon or sardines are eaten, they are a source of calcium: true/false.

92 Which of the following is correct?
Fish is a more valuable source of protein than meat.
Fish is equally valuable as a source of protein as meat.
Fish is a less valuable source of protein than meat.
Fish is not a source of protein at all.

93 The oil in oily fish is contained in the liver: true/false.

94 The carbohydrate in unripe fruit is in the form of . . . which changes to . . . when the fruit is ripe.

95 Which is the odd one out and why?
oranges, blackcurrants, lemons, avocado pears, strawberries, grapefruit.

96 Nuts are a source of cellulose: true/false.

97 Green vegetables are valuable because they contain which of the following vitamins and minerals?
Iron, calcium, vitamins A and C.
Phosphorus, calcium, vitamins A and D.
Iron, calcium, vitamins B and C.
Iodine, sodium, vitamins A and D.

98 Potatoes are a valuable source of vitamin D because they are eaten in large quantities: true/false.

99 State the main value of onions in cookery.

100 Which vitamin is contained in wholemeal flour?

101 Saccharine has no food value: true/false.

102 What food value have tea and coffee?

103 When compiling a balanced diet, what foods must be considered?

104 Food additives can be divided into which two categories?

105 **a** State the six materials known as nutrients and explain their purpose.
   b Define digestion and explain where and how it takes place.
   c Explain absorption stating where and how it occurs.
   d For each of the six nutrients state two foods containing each of the nutrients. Fully describe one of the nutrients.

106 **a** Explain the effects of cooking on nutrients.
   b Explain why some people require more food than others and explain the function of basal metabolism.
   c Describe a balanced diet and healthy eating.
   d Specify five guidelines for catering in institutions.
   e State six categories of additives; give an example of each.

ANSWERS

1 a liquid or solid substance which provides the body with materials for heat, energy, growth, repair and regulation of body processes

p197

2 proteins, carbohydrates, minerals, fats, vitamins, water   *p197*

3 nutrition   *p197*

4 sugar   *p197*

5 nutrition   *p197*

6 the breaking down of food in the body   *p197*

7 saliva – gastric juices   *p197*

8 true   *p197*

9   after food has been broken down   *p198*

10 smell, look and taste attractive   *p198*

11 when there is a lack of one or more nutrients   *p198*

12 *Energy*   *Growth and repair*   *Regulation of body*
                                              processes
    fats   protein   vitamins
    carbohydrates   minerals   minerals
    proteins   water   water   *p198*

13 animal, vegetable   *p199*

14 growth of the body and repair of body tissues   *p199*

15 yes   *p199*

16 more protein needed for growth, other adults need protein mainly
    for repair   *p199*

17 meat and fish, cheese and milk, bread and cereals, potatoes and
    pulses   *p199*

18 amino acids   *p200*

19 true   *p200*

20 amino acids   *p200*

21 onion, it is not a main source of protein   *p200*

22 true   *p200*

23 lightly cooked egg more easily digested than hard boiled egg *p200*

24 solid fat, oils   *p201*

25 protect vital organs of the body, provide heat and energy, some
    fats contain vitamins   *p201*

26 animal origin – butter, cod liver oil, suet, bacon, meat fat, lard,
    halibut liver oil, herring, cream, dripping, cheese
    vegetable origin – margarine, sunflower oil, soya bean, nuts,
    olive oil   *p201*

27 true   *p200*

28 blackcurrants, they do not provide protein   *p200*

29 fatty acids   *p201*

30 butyric (butter), stearic (e.g. beef suet), oleic (oils)   *p201*

31 texture and taste or flavour   *p201*

32 heat and energy   *p201*

33 herring, salmon, mackerel, pilchards, sardines, sprats   *p201*

34 sugar, starch, cellulose   *p202*

35 energy   *p202*

36 flour, sugar, cereals   *p202*

37 true   *p202*

38 maltose – grain
    lactose – milk
    sucrose – beet and cane sugar
    glucose – animal blood and honey
    fructose – fruit   *p202*

39 rice, flour, peas, butter beans, apples   *p202*

40 whole grains – rice, barley, tapioca
    powdered grains – flour, cornflour, ground rice
    vegetables – potatoes, parsnips, peas
    unripe fruit – bananas, apples, cooking pears
    cereals – cornflakes, shredded wheat etc.
    cooked starch – cakes, biscuits, sponges
    pasta – macaroni, spaghetti, vermicelli   *p202*

41 coarser structure of vegetables and cereals   *p204*

42 roughage in the intestine   *p204*

43 dietary fibre   *p204*

44 vital or essential for life   *p204*

45 true   *p204*

46 to help growth of children, to protect against disease   *p204*

47 liver, butter, herrings, carrots, apricots, cheese, milk   *p204*

48 true   *p204*

49 assist children's growth, helps body resist infection, enables better
    vision in the dark   *p204*

50 vitamin D   *p205*

51 A and D *p205*

52 sunlight *p205*

53 fish liver oil, dairy produce, fats *p205*

54 yes *p205*

55 yeast, liver, bacon, meat extract, oatmeal, cheese, kidney *p205*

56 Thiamin, Riboflavin, Nicotinic acid *p205*

57 yes *p205*

58 wholemeal bread T, cheese R, eggs R, bacon T, liver R, kidney N, yeast R, meat extract R N, peas T, beef N, oatmeal T, brewers yeast T R *p205*

59 Nicotinic acid *p205*

60 storage *p206*

61 blackcurrants, strawberries, grapefruit, potatoes, lemons, tomatoes, sprouts and other greens, oranges, banana *p206*

62 egg yolk – D
kidney – A
oranges – C
yeast – B *p206*

63 calcium, iron, iodine *p207*

64

Calcium	*Iron*	*Iodine*
milk	offal	foods from the sea
tinned fish bones	egg yolk	vegetables grown near
wholemeal bread	fish	the sea
green vegetables	wholemeal flour	drinking water
	green vegetables	obtained near the sea
		Iodised salt *p207*

65 vitamin D *p207*

66 milk, bones of tinned fish, cheese *p207*

67 calcium *p207*

68 calcium and vitamin D *p208*

69 liver, cheese, eggs, fish *p208*

70 oxygen and carbon dioxide *p208*

71 lean meat, offal, egg yolk   *p208*

72 sodium   *p208*

73 sodium   *p208*

74 metabolism, absorption, digestion, body fluids, excretion,
    secretion   *p208*

75 fruits, vegetables, meat, eggs, fish, offal   *p209*

76 protein – over-cooking reduces nutritive value
    carbohydrate – needs to be thoroughly cooked
    fat – not affected by normal cooking
    iron – may be acquired from pan
    vitamin B – destroyed by high temperature and bi-carb
    vitamin C – lost by cooking and keeping hot   *p209*

77 it can do, e.g. lightly cooked protein is easier to digest and
    therefore has greater value nutritively than over-cooked protein
                                                                            p209

78 true   *p209*

79 no   *p209*

80 A and D   *p210*

81 to enable heart to beat, blood circulate, lungs etc. to function; for
    every activity   *p210*

82 **a** energy value
    b energy value   *p210*

83 calorie, kilojoule   *p211*

84 true   *p211*

85 young male   *p211*

86 milk   *p211*

87 because of additional vitamins A and D which may be low in
    butter in winter   *p214*

88 contains concentrated nutrients   *p214*

89 thiamin   *p215*

90 false, cheaper cuts of meat are as nourishing as dearer cuts   *p215*

91 true   *p215*

92 fish is equally as valuable as meat   *p215*

93 false – the oil is contained in the flesh   *p215*

94 starch to sugar   *p215*

95 avocado pears contain fat   *p216*

96 true   *p216*

97 iron, calcium, vitamins A and C   *p216*

98 false, they are valuable, because of the small amount of vitamin C
they contain, due to large quantities eaten   *p217*

99 provision of flavour   *p217*

100 vitamin B   *p217*

101 true   *p217*

102 the value of the milk and sugar used in tea or coffee *p217*

103 body building, energy producing and protective foods   *p218*

104 natural and synthetic   *p219*

105 a proteins, fats, carbohydrates, vitamins, minerals, water – heat
and energy, growth and repair, regulation of body
processes   *pp197–98*
  b breaking down of food in the mouth, stomach, small intestine
aid of juices – saliva, gastric
  c absorbed into blood stream in stomach, small and large intestine
through stomach lining
  d protein – meat, fish, eggs, cheese etc.
fat – butter, oil, margarine etc.
carbohydrates – bread, cereals, sugar etc.
vitamins – fish liver, green vegetables etc.
minerals – bread, milk, liver etc.
water – drinks, fruit, vegetables etc.
e.g. water
    required for: body fluids, metabolism, secretion, temperature
    regulation, absorption, excretion, digestion
    sources: drinks, fruit, vegetables, combination of fats,
    carbohydrates, protein   *pp197–209*

106 a protein – coagulates, shrinks
cabohydrates – granules swell enabling digestion
fat – not affected

minerals – loss in liquid
vitamin A and D – not lost
vitamin B – destroyed by high temperatures
vitamin C – lost by cooking   *p209*
b energy requirements vary: men more than women, young more
than old, energetic work – sedentary work
basal metabolism – amount of energy to maintain body
functions, keep warm, 1700 calories (kj) required daily   *p211*
c amount: adequate of all nutrients
                no omissions, no excesses
                mixture
limit: salt, sugar, alcohol, fat
increase: fibre, cereals, vegetables   *p218*
d calorie spread, protein twice a day, fruit daily, vegetables daily,
high fibre cereals, minimum salt, grill rather than fry   *p219*
e preservatives – salt, sugar, vinegar, synthetics
colouring – cochineal, caramel, synthetics
flavouring – chemical e.g. monosodium glutamate
sweetening – saccharin, sorbitol etc.
emulsifying – lecithin, G.M.S.
antioxidants – vitamin E
flour improvers – vitamin C
thickeners – gelatine, agar-agar, synthetics
humectants – glycerine
nutrients – A and D   *p219*

Food preservation

QUESTIONS

1   Name three micro-organisms.

2   When whiskers form on food they are called . . .

3   On which three foods are whiskers likely to grow?

4   Are all micro-organisms destructive?

5   How may most micro-organisms be checked and how may they be
    killed?

6   Explain the reason for your answer to the previous question.

7   Dry foods and those containing a high percentage of sugar or vinegar are less likely to go bad: true/false.

8   Enzymes are chemical substances produced by living cells: true/false.

9   Fruits are ripened by the action of . . .

10 When meat is hung it becomes tender due to . . .

11 If enzyme activity goes too far foods can be spoiled: true/false.

12 What scale is used to measure food acidity and alkalinity?

13 What must be done to prevent enzyme activity from going too far?

14 Which is the correct way to write the term for the degree of acidity of a food material?
     pH, HP, Ph, ph.

15 What numbers on the range of acidity and alkalinity would you give to
     lemons, banana, egg white.

16 The browning of cut apples and bananas is caused by enzymes: true/false.

17 What is the effect of lemon juice on cut bananas and apples?

18 Name eight ways of preserving food.

19 Drying and dehydration of food is achieved by extracting the m . . . from the food.

20 The drying of foods prevents the growth of what three things?

21 Originally foods were dried in the sun: true/false.

22 What is the modern process of freezing and drying?
     accelerated freeze drying, quick frozen drying, deep frozen drying, frozen and dried

23 Give three advantages of dried food.

24 Name six foods preserved by drying.

25 Little flavour or food value is lost in the drying of food: true/false.

26 Which is the odd one out and why?
     currants, strawberries, sultanas, apricots, prunes.

27 Can eggs and milk be dried?

28 Explain in a *few* words the roller and spray processes.

29 Are micro-organisms in food killed by refrigeration?

30 Cold storage of fresh foods retards the decay of food, it does not prevent it from going bad: true/false.

31 Quick freezing is satisfactory because
   medium ice crystals are formed in the food cells
   large ice crystals are formed in the food cells
   small ice crystals are formed in the food cells
   small ice crystals are formed outside the food cells.

32 Meat kept in a temperature just above freezing point is known as c . . . meat.

33 The meat referred to in the previous questions will keep for up to 1 month, 2 months, 3 months, 6 months.

34 Why are lamb carcasses sometimes frozen but not beef carcasses?

35 Both raw and cooked meats can be quick frozen: true/false.

36 State four advantages for using frozen raw foods.

37 State four advantages for using pre-cooked frozen foods.

38 What is meant by a 'blown' can?
   One that has a slight dent.
   One that has no label.
   One that had air blown in during processing.
   One with a bulge at either end.

39 What should be done with blown cans?

40 Where is the correct place to store tinned ham?
   in the deep freeze, in the refrigerator, in the larder, a cool part of the kitchen.

41 Tinned food will keep indefinitely: true/false.

42 List the following can sizes in order of size – largest first.
   A2, A10, 14Z, A1, A2½.

43 What is the advantage of preserving meat and fish by salting and smoking?

44 Name two meats preserved by salting or pickling.

45 In what is meat pickled?
   brine, vinaigrette, vinegar, spiced vinegar.

46 Name four fish preserved by salting and pickling.

47 What is brine?
stock containing saltpetre, water containing iron, a salt
court bouillon, a salt solution.

48 What is the effect of adding salt to butter and margarine?

49 Name four items preserved because of the sugar content.

50 If too little sugar is used when making jam, what will be the effect
on the keeping quality?

51 Name six foods preserved in vinegar.

52 Match the item with a method of preservation.
glacé   salmon
crystallised   peel
candied   onions
pickled   angelica
smoked   sultanas
dried   cherries

53 Name a substitute for wheat flour for use in thickening foods to be
deep-frozen.

54 **a** State two foods with a high acidity level and two with a high
alkalinity.
b Describe how foods may be preserved and state twelve
preservation methods.
c Explain in detail one method of preservation and list foods
preserved by this method.

55 What advantages does irradiation have over heating, chilling and
chemical preservation methods?

56 What is modified atmospheric packaging?

57 How does MAP preserve food?

ANSWERS _____

1 moulds, yeasts, bacteria   *p220*

2 moulds   *p220*

3 sweet foods, meat, cheese   *p220*

4 no, e.g. some flavour cheese such as Stilton   *p220*

5 refrigeration, heat   *p220*

6 low temperature retards growth, high temperature kills micro-
        organisms   *p220*

7 true   *p221*

8 true   *p221*

9 enzymes   *p221*

10 enzymes   *p221*

11 true   *p221*

12 the scale is pH range 1–14   *p221*

13 refrigerated or heated to a high temperature   *p221*

14 the correct way is pH   *p221*

15 lemons – 1, banana – 4, egg white – 10   *p221*

16 true   *p221*

17 prevents browning   *p221*

18 drying, bottling, smoking, radiation, chilling, pickling, chemical,
        vacuum packing, freezing, salting, gas storage   *p222*

19 moisture   *p223*

20 moulds, yeasts, bacteria   *p223*

21 true   *p223*

22 accelerated freeze drying   *p223*

23 keep indefinitely if kept dry, minimum storage space required,
        easily transported, no waste, easily stored, accurate cost and
        portion control   *p223*

24 vegetables, herbs, eggs, milk, coffee, fruits, meat, fish *p223*

25 true – other than vitamin C   *p223*

26 strawberries are not dried   *p223*

27 yes   *p224*

28 Roller – food poured onto heated rollers causing evaporation then
        scraped off
        spray – fine jet sprayed into hot air and water evaporated *p224*

29	no, they are dormant	*p224*
30	true	*p224*
31	small crystals formed in the food cells	*p225*
32	chilled	*p225*
33	one month	*p225*
34	due to size of beef carcass – time taken to freeze and to thaw would adversely affect texture of the meat	*p225*
35	true	*p227*
36	foods always in season, guaranteed quality, little loss of vitamin C, ready prepared, compact storage, simple cost and portion control	*p227*
37	labour saving, ease of costing and control, reduced kitchen space and equipment needed, no wastage	*p227*
38	bulge at both ends	*p227*
39	discarded	*p227*
40	in the refrigerator	*p227*
41	false – storage time varies with product	*p227*
42	A10, A2½, A2, 14Z, A1	*p228*
43	varied dishes and flavour can be put on menu	*p228*
44	silverside, ox tongues	*p228*
45	brine	*p228*
46	salmon, trout, haddock, herring	*p229*
47	a salt solution	*p228*
48	acts as a preservative	*p228*
49	jams, jellies, candied, crystallised, glacé fruits	*p229*
50	it will not keep for long	*p228*
51	gherkins, capers, onions, red cabbage, pickles, chutneys	*p229*
52	glacé – cherries crystallised – angelica candied – peel pickled – onions smoked – salmon dried – sultanas	*pp228–29*

53 tapioca or maize starch   *p226*

54 **a** high acidity: lemons, vinegar
     high alkalinity: mineral water, egg whites   *p221*
  b remove moisture – drying, dehydration
     make cold – chill, freeze
     apply heat – can, bottle
     radiation – X, gamma rays
     chemical – salting, pickling
     vacuum
     drying, chilling, freezing, canning, bottling, salting, smoking,
     chemical, gas storage, radiation, pickling, vacuum   *p222*
  c e.g. sugar: high concentration of sugar prevents growth of
     moulds, yeasts and bacteria
     crystallised – candied then allowed to crystallise – violet
     candied – saturated heavy syrup, dried – peels
     glacé – candied then dipped – cherries
     also jams, marmalades, jellies   *p222*

55 Irradiation works well with frozen or heat sensitive products.
It does not cause any significant increase in temperature; packaged
products can be sterilised in the final pack, thus preventing
contamination; irradiation has a minimal import on the nutritional
value of the food; proteins and carbohydrates are unaffected;
irradiation processing is a clean technology. No chemical additives
are used on residues left behind in the food and the process does
not contaminate or damage the environment

56 modified atmosphere packaging (MAP) is a flexible way of
extending the shelf life of many kinds of fresh foods up to two or
three times the normal levels

57 MAP involves replacing the normal surrounding or dead space
atmosphere within food packages with specific mixtures of gases.
Its objectives are to inhibit the growth of pathogenic bacteria and
moulds and to extend the shelf lives of certain chilled food
products.

PRODUCT DEVELOPMENT (CHEMISTRY IN THE KITCHEN)

Read pp233–52 of *The Theory of Catering*.

QUESTIONS

1   What is the pH of pure water?

2   What is the pH of distilled water?

3   How many different amino acids are found in proteins?

4   A typical protein may contain 550 amino acids: true/false.

5   Name the two protein shapes.

6   Protein can be denatured by acid: true/false.

7   What is an enzyme?

8   What do bees produce honey from?

9   Why is sugar necessary for the addition of pectin?

10   Where is starch produced from?

11   What are pectins used for?

12   What are lipids?

13   Why are lipids important in food production?

14   Give two examples of saturated fatty acids and two examples of polyunsaturated fats.

15   Most fats contain at least five different sorts of fatty acids in their make up: true/false.

16   Butyric acid is the most important of all fatty acids occurring in fats: true/false.

17   What is an antioxidant?

18   Name one naturally occurring antioxidant and one artificial?

19   What do emulsifiers do?

20   Give examples of emulsifiers.

21 Give examples of the types of taste.

22 Where are taste preferences first learnt?

23 Give an example of a flavour enhancer.

24 People are most sensitive to taste when the food is between 22° and 41°C: true/false.

25 Briefly describe what is meant by mouth feel.

26 State the various ways in which proteins can be denatured.

27 Explain the effect heat has on the fibrous protein in a fillet steak.

28 State the effect of acid on milk.

29 Gluten is formed by two proteins – gliadin and glutenin. Explain the effect gluten has in bread dough.

30 What part do enzymes play in the ageing of meat?

31 State the effect sugar has on baked goods.

32 What is the effect of water on starch granules?

33 Name four factors which affect the thickening capacity of starches.

34 A firm pectin gel relies on a number of conditions, list these conditions.

35 What are the purposes of lipids in culinary work?

36 State the effect on fats and oils if their quality is not maintained.

37 Explain how oxidation causes rancidity in fats and oils.

38 **a** State what you understand by the term emulsion.
  b The emulsion depends on three main factors, what are they?

39 Sugar is an example of the sweet taste we experience; give examples of other taste sensations we experience in sensory evaluation.

40 Give examples of the different textures that an individual may experience during food evaluation.

ANSWERS

1	7.0	p233
2	5.5	p233

3   20   *p233*

4   true   *p233*

5   fibrous and globular   *p234*

6   true   *p235*

7   an enzyme is a protein, which acts as a catalyst   *p238*

8   nectar   *p240*

9   sugar necessary to achieve the setting action   *p240*

10   plants   *p241*

11   pectins are used to set jams, jellies and commercial desserts   *p242*

12   lipids are fats, oils, cholesterol and certain emulsifying agents   *p243*

13   lipids contribute to the eating quality of cakes, pastries, biscuits;
they also affect the texture of yeast products by separating the
gluten layers and pastry making by shortening the gluten strands

                                                                             p243

14   palm oil, coconut oil, butter, beef fat, mutton fat, lard   *p245*

15   true   *p245*

16   false, it is oleic acid   *p245*

17   they slow down the development of fat oxidation   *p246*

18   vitamin E
butylated hydroxyanisole (BHA)   *p246*

19   emulsifiers stabilise dispersion of the immiscible liquids   *p246*

20   proteins, plant gums, resins, starch   *p246*

21   sweet, salt, butter, sour, metallic, soapy   *p251*

22   childhood   *p251*

23   monosodium glutamate   *p251*

24   true   *p251*

25   consistency, chewiness, brittleness, crunchiness, etc.   *p252*

26   heat during normal cooking methods, salting, mechanical action,
enzymes, acid   *p235*

27 when fillet steak is cooked the protein called myosin coagulates at 71°C (160°F); if the temperature continues to increase, the protein contracts, squeezes out much of the water associated with it and thus becomes drier and the eating quality is impaired   *p236*

28 if acid is added to milk, hydrogen ions are added; these are positively charged particles. The hydrogen ions (positively charged) are attracted to the albumen globules (negatively charged) and the two neutralise each other; the albumen is then electrically neutral and any globules that come into contact stick together or coagulate and form a mass with a gel-like, semi solid consistency   *p237*

29 gluten gives bread dough its elasticity and plasticity; during kneading the gluten molecules are physically rearranged from a tangled mass to a series of parallel sheets; the molecules in the sheets of gluten are shaped like tiny springs and account for the stretchy nature of the bread dough; the sheets of gluten act to trap the gas formed by the yeast growing in the dough and allow the bread to rise   *p237*

30 meat benefits from a period of ageing or slow chemical change, before it is consumed; the flavour improves and it becomes more tender; as lactic acid accumulates in the tissues after slaughter, it begins to break down the walls of lysosomes, the cell bodies that store protein, attacking enzymes; as a result, these enzymes will digest proteins indiscriminately; lactic acid breaks down the structures in the cells that contain enzymes capable of digesting protein   *p239*

31 sugar is used as a sweetener and will also give volume to baked goods, ice cream, jams and confectionery; it also assists in the leavening of some cakes by assisting the incorporation of air; air is incorporated into cakes making during the creaming process by the physical action of the sugar crystals dragging pockets of air into the fat; if the sugar crystals are too large, few pockets of air will be incorporated   *p240*

32 when starch granules are mixed with cold water they will only absorb water and swell to a limited extent; the water cannot penetrate between the strongly attached starch chains; as the water is heated, the molecules of water move more rapidly and thus begin to penetrate the starch grains; the water causes the grain to swell; as swelling occurs the mixture thickens; some of the starch

molecules burst out from the granule and form a tangled mass that
contributes to the thickening process *p241*

33 **a** the type of starch used is important; high amylose starches have
better thickening properties because of the one chain like
molecules which are less likely to become tangled than the
compact amylopectin molecules
b the thickening properties are changed by heat treatment
c sugar decreases the thickness of starch thickened fillings *p241*

34 percentage of pectin
molecule weight of the pectin
percentage of methyl ester groups
amount of sugar *p242*

35 lipids provide heat transfer
cooking medium
texture
emulsification
flavour *p243*

36 fats and oils deteriorate because of odours – many compounds that
have a strong aroma can dissolve fats; if the fats are stored in an
open container they are able to absorb these odours; also, rancidity
– this is caused by the presence of free fatty acids which have an
unpleasant smell *pp243–44*

37 this involves the reaction of unsaturated fatty acids with oxygen to
release small fatty acids and other molecules that affect the flavour
and aroma; the development of rancidity by hydrolysis or
oxidation occurs faster under certain conditions *p245*

38 **a** an emulsion is a stable dispersion of an oil and water
b the composition of the oil and water phase
the chemical nature of the emulsifying agent
the proportions of the oil and water present *p246*

39 salt – sodium chloride
butter – alkaloids
sour – acids, vinegar, lemon juice
metallic – potassium chloride in some salt substitutes
soapy – after taste in baking powder goods *pp248–51*

40 texture, elastic, crumbly, creamy, liquid, viscous, lumpy, crisp,
crunchiness, soft, hard *p252*

MENU PLANNING

Read pp253–81 of *The Theory of Catering*.

Read pp253–81 of *The Theory of Catering*.

QUESTIONS

See introduction, for note on this Chapter

1   What are the two functions of a menu?

2   Give two ways in which a caterer can be guilty of an offence under the Trade Descriptions Act.

3   The Trade Descriptions Act is concerned with
      a clear account of the trade practised
      an accurate description of the item offered for sale
      a description of the various jobs in the trade
      an accurate account of the trades union.

4   If 'eggs and bacon' were stated on the menu, should one or more than one egg be served?

5   It would be a contravention of the Trade Descriptions Act to write on the menu 'fillet of haddock' and serve fillet of cod: true/false.

6   What is the main difference between a *table d'hôte* and an *à la carte* menu?

7   Would you consider cheese soufflé and grilled steak suitable items for a large banquet? Gives reasons for your answer.

8   When are menu cards usually given to hospital patients?

9   Suggest three reasons why it is in the interest of progressive companies to offer a good catering service for their employees?

10 Name two important factors that should be considered when preparing meals for school children.

11 What is a *cyclical* menu?

12 Give two advantages and two disadvantages of cyclical menus?

13 Name the two main departments whose availability and skill must be considered when planning a menu.

14 The aim of menu planning is to give customers what they want, not what the caterer thinks they want: true/false.

15 The traditional name given to a set menu at a set price is
   à la carte, chef's selection, meal of the day, table d'hôte.

16 An *à la carte* menu is one
   for customers wanting a set menu
   where it is served from a buffet or cart
   where the dishes are individually priced
   used at a call order unit.

17 State six important points that should be taken into consideration
   before planning a menu.

18 Give two reasons why it is sensible to use foods in season.

19 What are the problems of planning menus without giving
   consideration to the kitchen equipment available?

20 Why should the capabilities of the serving staff be considered when
   selecting the dishes and plates on which food is served?

21 What is understood by *menu balance*?

22 Criticise the following menus.
   a Mushroom Soup
      Filets of Sole Bonne Femme
      Boiled Chicken and Rice
      Mushroom and Bacon Savoury
   b Tomato Soup
      Fillets of Sole Dugléré
      Hungarian Goulash
      Marquise Potatoes
      Stuffed Tomatoes
      Strawberry Flan
   c Potato Soup
      Fricassée of Veal
      Buttered Turnips
      Creamed Potatoes
      Meringue and Vanilla Ice-cream

23 State six common faults in menu planning.

24 What do you understand by *plate appeal*?

25 Give two examples of plated foods to illustrate your answer to the
   previous question.

26 *Brunoise* means
   small neat dice, basic brown sauce, braising, browning.

27 *Contrefilet* is a
    large fillet steak, small fillet steak, boned wing rib of beef, boned
    sirloin of beef.

28 *Navarin* is a
    navy dish of pork and beans, brown lamb or mutton stew,
    Normandy speciality of tripe, Northern France pancake.

29 *Ragoût* means
    grill, boil, stew, fried.

30 Which is correct?
    hors-d'oeuvres variés, hors-d'oeuvre variés, hor-d'oeuvres varié,
    hor-d'oeuvre variés.

31 If the house policy is to write all menus in English what would you
    do with
    mayonnaise, hors-d'oeuvre, consommé

32 Chicken Sauté Parmentier has a garnish of
    turned potatoes, duchesse potatoes, 1cm dice potatoes, sauté
    potatoes.

33 Compile a four course menu illustrating good balance of texture,
    food value, colour etc.

34 Which way do you prefer to see this item on the menu? Give your
    reason why.
    Poached Turbot with Hollandaise Sauce.
    Sea fresh succulent Turbot with Dutch butter sauce.
    Turbot Poché Sauce Hollandaise.
    Turbot Poché Sauce Hollandaise (Boiled Turbot and
    Hollandaise Sauce).

35 Match these items.

Condé	coffee
Washington	tomatoes
Véronique	sweetcorn
Doria	cucumber
Mornay	cauliflower
Portugaise	cheese
Moka	rice
Dubarry	grapes

36 Trout meunière Bretonne is shallow fried trout garnished with
    capers and lemon segments
    turned pieces of cucumber

soft roes, mushrooms and tomato
shrimps and sliced mushrooms.

37 What flavour would *Suchard* indicate on the menu?

38 Praline ice-cream would contain what ingredient?

39 In sweet dishes what ingredient is indicated by these terms?
    Chantilly, Normande, Montmorency, Melba, Hélène.

40 What ingredient is indicated by the use of these words?
    Clamart, Lyonnaise, Florentine, Princesse.

41 What is the difference between a traditional English breakfast and
    a continental breakfast?

42 List three points to consider when compiling a breakfast menu.

43 At which meal would these dishes most likely be served?
    Indicate B for breakfast, L for lunch and D for dinner.
        egg and bacon,   boiled beef and carrots,   treacle pudding,
        suprême de volaille,   rice pudding,   kipper,   sorbet,
        liver and bacon.

44 Suggest three first courses suitable for the lunch menu in a
    medium priced hotel in summer.

45 Would these dishes usually be offered for luncheon or dinner?
        braised oxtail, steak and kidney pudding, chicken casserole,
        braised sweetbreads, Irish stew, hot pot.

46 Suggest three light English sweets available for a works canteen
    menu in summer.

47 Suggest a typical three course English luncheon menu for a party
    of overseas visitors on their first visit to England.

48 The party in the previous question, who had an early breakfast and
    a light lunch, require a real English tea. What would you offer
    them?

49 Suggest eight suitable items for a dish of French pastries.

50 Name four popular items that may be served toasted for tea.

51 Suggest three interesting first courses for dinner at a commercial
    hotel in winter.

52 Indicate the fish which are more suitable for dinner menus than
    lunch menus.
        cod, herring, sole, salmon trout.

53 A *sorbet* is a
type of sauce, type of vegetable, lightly frozen water ice, a double sized sausage.

54 Suggest three interesting sweets suitable for hospital patients on a normal diet in winter.

55 Suggest a four course dinner menu for 24 very important people to be served in November with no expense spared.

56 In April the annual office party for 100 people requires a light supper at 11pm. What would you offer them?

57 Match these items.
roast   macaroni au gratin
savoury   egg mayonnaise
pasta   Welsh rarebit
hors-d'oeuvre   best end of lamb

58 On which courses of the menu would these dishes be placed?
cheese soufflé, raised pie, whitebait, camembert, potted shrimps.

59 State two important points to be considered when compiling a banquet menu.

60 Why should heavily garnished dishes be avoided for banquets?

61 Can banquets be offered for both luncheon and dinner?

62 Name four different occasions for buffets and four types of buffet.

63 Suggest a menu for one of the buffets named in the previous answer, for 250 people at Christmas in a moderately priced seaside hotel.

64 What is an essential requirement for food prepared for a fork buffet?

65 It is usual to serve canapés as one of the varieties of foods at cocktail parties: true/false.

66 Suggest six interesting canapés.

67 What size should canapés be?

68 Name six items of a savoury nature suitable for a buffet.

69 **a** There are several kinds of menu; select three and explain how, and for whom, they are used.
b Explain eight considerations to be taken into account prior to planning a menu.

    c Describe twelve factors to consider when compiling a menu.

70 **a** Suggest a suitable continental and full breakfast menu for an English three star hotel.

    b State four cold dishes and four cold sweet dishes suitable for service in a hospital during the summer. Give reasons for your choice.

    c Specify four hot dishes and four hot sweets suitable for service in winter for an industrial catering establishment. Give reasons for your choice.

    d Compile a dinner menu for a coming of age party for 40 people in June.

71 What is understood by the term *menu development* in relation to planning a catering operation?

72 State the factors which have to be taken into account when planning a 'healthy eating' menu.

ANSWERS

1	inform staff what is to be prepared inform customers what is available	*p257*
2	applies a false description to goods supplies or offers to supply goods falsely described	*p257*
3	an accurate description of the item offered for sale	*p257*
4	more than one	*p257*
5	true	*p258*
6	table d'hôte – set menu at a set price à la carte – the dishes are individually priced	*p258*
7	no; soufflés – delicate, must be served as soon as cooked or they sink, difficult for large numbers; steaks need to be cooked to different degrees according to customers wishes; problem with large numbers	*p278*
8	usually the day before meal is required	*p254*
9	convenience for staff, provision of good food, to attract and retain staff, well fed workers work better, good employer image etc.	*p255*

10 nutritional balance, healthy eating, appropriate to children, suitable choice   *p255*

11 compiled to cover a period of time e.g. one month then used again   *p255*

12 e.g. advantages: time saved compiling menu, printing costs reduced, ordering, preparation, presentation and service skills increased
disadvantages: repetition, weather and seasonal effects, customers require changes, staleness of staff and customers   *p255*

13 kitchen and restaurant

14 true

15 table d'hôte   *p254*

16 individually priced dishes   *p254*

17 establishment location, competition, type of establishment, customer requirements, supplies and storage, spending power, size of menu, equipment, labour capability, costs   *p260*

18 better quality, cheaper, readily available, no storage   *p261*

19 e.g. overloading of equipment, bottlenecks, staff frustration, customers kept waiting

20 appropriate to their technical skill, weight of dishes, size of dishes, number of items to serve, difficult items to handle, time to serve, temperature of food, appearance of food to customer   *p261*

21 balanced texture, taste, ingredients, colour, flavour, sauces   *p261*

22 **a** repetition of mushroom
b repetition of red
c repetition of white

23 repetition of ingredients, colour, texture; inadequate choice – healthy eating, nutritional balance, capabilities of staff not considered etc.

24 when food on plate looks appetising and smells good – not too much or too little – colourful – neatly arranged

25 e.g. cold meat and salad – crisp lettuce, neatly cut tomatoes, cucumber and beetroot, watercress, quarters of hard boiled egg, neatly arranged with sliced roast beef and ham

26 small neat dice

27 boned sirloin of beef   *p265*

28 brown lamb or mutton stew   *p267*

29 stew   *p268*

30 hors-d'oeuvre variés   *p267*

31 do not attempt to translate mayonnaise or hors-d'oeuvre but you may translate consommé as clear soup if you wish

32 diced potatoes

33 consider points stated on pp261–62

34 all four are acceptable; are you influenced by considering type of establishment, preference for English or French, simplicity?

35 Condé – rice
     Washington – sweetcorn
     Véronique – grapes
     Doria – cucumber
     Mornay – cheese
     Portugaise – tomatoes
     Moka – coffee
     Dubarry – cauliflower

36 capers and lemon segments

37 chocolate

38 crushed nut toffee

39 cream, apples, cherries, raspberries, pears

40 peas, onions, spinach, asparagus

41 English breakfast – includes cereals and cooked items e.g. eggs and bacon, kipper etc.
     continental – croissants or rolls, preserves and coffee
     several courses for English breakfast   *p271*

42 continental or English, wide choice – muesli, cereals, eggs, bacon, ham, kipper, haddock, yoghurt, fruit, suitable for breakfast, table d'hôte or à la carte   *p271*

43 egg and bacon – B, boiled beef – L, treacle pudding – L, Suprême de volaille – D/L, rice pudding – L, kipper – B, sorbet – L/D, liver and bacon – L

44 e.g. hors-d'oeuvre, melon, mushroom soup   *pp271–72*

45 lunch

46 e.g. apple pie, sponge pudding, fruit and ice cream

47 e.g. smoked mackerel
    roast beef, Yorkshire pudding
    roast potatoes, spring greens
    bread and butter pudding

48 e.g. scones with jam, Cornish cream, e.g. Eccles cakes, Bath buns,
    Chelsea buns, jam tarts, mincemeat tarts, shortbread, cherry cakes,
    Queen cakes etc., sandwiches

49 e.g. éclairs, cream slice, gâteaux, cream buns, fruit tartlets, cream
    horns, fruit slice, palmier

50 tea cakes, toast, buns, crumpets, muffins

51 e.g. minestrone, spaghetti bolognaise, curried eggs

52 sole and salmon trout

53 lightly frozen water ice

54 e.g. fruit sponge, rice pudding, jam sauce, fruit salad

55 consider expensive items, menu balance, imported foods out of
    season; caviar, smoked salmon, game birds, venison, asparagus,
    strawberries, exotic foods

56 consider time of day, therefore not heavy foods – clear soup, cold
    foods, salads, grills, fruit salad, gâteaux

57 savoury – Welsh rarebit
    roast – best end of lamb
    pasta – macaroni au gratin
    hors-d'oeuvre – egg mayonnaise

58 cheese soufflé – last course
    raised pie, cold buffet – main
    whitebait – first course
    camembert – cheese course
    potted shrimps – first course

59 cooking facilities, suitable dishes, serving staff   *p278*

60 problems of serving   *p278*

61 yes   *p278*

62 i wedding, coming of age, anniversary, retirement, conference
                                                                                  p278
    ii light (e.g. cocktail) fork, hot, cold, hot and cold

63 consider: hot or cold dishes, or both, how served – buffet or sat
    down, seasonal dishes, choice, cost etc.

64 small size of items easily handled with a fork

65 true

66 anchovies, sardines, pâté, egg, smoked salmon, salami, cheese etc.

67 about size of 10p piece

68 quiche, salmon mousse, Scotch eggs, galantines, paté, chipolatas,
    patties

69 **a** select from: à la carte, function, table d'hôte, ethnic or
      speciality, hospital, industrial, children's, old people's etc.;
      e.g. à la carte – individual prices of dishes, cooked to order, size
      of portion, scope of courses
      restaurant service – customer may have to wait for dish to be
      cooked, prepared to pay for this service
      examples of à la carte dishes: grilled steaks, omelets, grilled fish,
      asparagus, whitebait

    b select from
        location – need to include local foods
                – competition in the area
        customers – suited to their needs
                – spending power
                – food trends and fashions
        menu – type
                – range of dishes
        equipment – kitchen and restaurant
        staff – ability, availability
        supplies – storage, availability
        cost – to make profit or keep within budget

    c select from: type of establishment, customer – religion,
      vegetarian, time of year, price range, foods in season, number of
      courses, special dishes, sequence of courses, time of day, menu
      language, nutritional balance, no repetition of commodities,
      wines, colour, flavours, texture of courses

70 a examples on use of menus
    b points to consider: hospital – dishes to look appetising, suitable
       for service to bed patients, cost within the budget, nutritionally
       suitable, light in texture, not heavy
       summer – use foods in season, variety of ingredients
       e.g. tuna salad, chicken mayonnaise, Scotch egg and salad,
       cheese salad, fruit yoghurt, apple pie, ice cream and jelly, pear
       condé
    c points to consider: industrial catering – dishes for men and
       women, suitable sized portions, cost according to policy, variety
       of ingredients
       winter – substantial items as well as light seasonal foods
       e.g. fish pie, steak and kidney pudding, vegetarian moussaka,
       curried eggs, bread and butter pudding, sultana sponge
       pudding, fruit pie, apple fritters
    d points to consider: items suitable for dinner, for June, in season,
       the occasion – special, age of majority attending, vegetarian
       alternative, set or limited choice, style of service – buffet, plated,
       etc., any special diets, etc.

Menu example

> **Smoked Salmon**
> **Breast of Chicken with Asparagus**
> **French Beans**
> **New Rissolée Potatoes**
> **Strawberry Vacherin and Vanilla Ice Cream**

alternative

> **Ratatouille Pancakes**
> **served with a light cheese sauce**

71 consider: customer needs, location, market – types of customer
    aiming to attract, average spending of these customers, type of
    menu that will attract group or groups you are focusing on,
    equipment and kitchen design, type of restaurant operation,
    restaurant design, theme if required, staff required – level of skill,
    volume, number of covers, break even point, profit margins

72 develop each of these points: customers, calorific value matched to
    customer needs, fat – saturated, unsaturated, fibre, sugar, salt

FOOD PURCHASING, STORAGE AND CONTROL

Read pp282–317 of *The Theory of Catering*.

QUESTIONS

1 State the objective of writing standard recipes.

2 List the advantages of an efficient costing system.

3 Name four factors which affect the profitability of the establishment.

4 What is essential when purchasing commodities?

5 Which guide to purchasing should be followed?
   The cheapest is the best.
   Compare quality with price.
   The dearest is always the best.
   The best quality is the cheapest.

6 List ten points which assist in the efficient buying of food.

7 Out-of-date price lists should be consulted: true/false.

8 What do you understand by *portion control*?

9 Why should portion control be linked closely with the buying of food?

10 Better quality food usually gives a better yield than inferior quality food: true/false.

11 What is the golden rule to use when considering portion control?

12 Indicate which points should be considered regarding portion control.
   The type of customer or establishment.
   The Safety at Work Act.
   The quality of the food.
   The qualifications of the kitchen staff.
   The buying price of the food.
   The gas and electricity services available.

13 Name six items of equipment that can assist portion control.

14 Approximately how many portions of soup would be obtained from a litre?

1–2, 3–4, 4–6, 7–8.

15 Approximately how many portions of haddock would be obtained from 1kg of haddock fillet?

2, 4, 6, 8.

16 Approximately how many portions would be obtained from 1 litre of custard?

16–24, 25–30, 32–36, 40–50.

17 Sausages are obtainable 12, 16 or 20 to the kg: true/false.

18 Approximately how many portions would be obtained from 1kg of unpeeled old potatoes?

2–3, 4–6, 7–8, 9–10.

19 How many sheep's kidneys would be a portion?

20 Briefly describe the differences between the following markets.

primary, secondary, tertiary.

21 What is a *standard purchasing specification*?

22 List three advantages of standard purchasing specifications.

23 Give two objectives of a standard recipe.

24 Outline three of the main difficulties of controlling food.

25 Suggest three factors that can affect a food control system.

26 What are the gaps in this control cycle of daily operation?

purchasing, storing, preparing.

27 For sales and volume forecasting to be of practical value what two things must the forecast predict?

28 List six factors which will affect the profitability of an establishment.

29 What are the advantages of an efficient costing system?

30 One costing system will suit any type of catering establishment: true/false.

31 What are the three main elements that make up the total cost of an item or a meal?

32 **a** What are food and materials costs known as?

b What are labour costs and overheads known as?

33 List six examples of overhead items.

34 What is gross profit or kitchen profit?

35 What is net profit?

36 **a** Sales minus food cost =?
   b Sales minus total cost =?
   c Food cost plus gross profit =?

37 Profit is expressed as a percentage of the . . . price.

38 Finding the food costs helps control costs, prices and profits: true/false.

39 Will an efficient food cost system help prevent waste and stealing?

40 Sales less food cost =
      gross profit, net profit, gross price, net price.

41 **a** State eight principles which relate to purchasing.
   b Who may be responsible for purchasing?
   c Where may foods be purchased?

42 Portion control.
   a Define portion control and explain its relevance to
      i   the type of customer and establishment
      ii the quality of the food
      iii the purchasing price of the food.
   b You are responsible for providing portion control equipment. What could you use for ice cream, soup? How could you ensure that all portions of meat served to the customer were the same?

43 **a** To achieve efficient purchasing, costing and control explain in what ways do standard purchasing specifications and standard recipes assist in achieving this aim?
   b What may cause the system to be less than 100% effective?

44 Costing.
   a State four advantages of an efficient costing system.
   b To make the system work, what is required?
   c Describe the three main elements of costing which affect an item or meal.

45 **a** Explain four of the difficulties in controlling food.
   b State five factors which affect a food control system.

  c There are five stages in the control cycle: briefly explain each.
  d Indicate eight reasons why the system may be adversely affected.

ANSWERS _____

1   the purpose of writing standard recipes is to determine the
     following
          the quantity and quality of ingredients to be used in stating the
          purchase specifications
          the yield obtainable from a recipe
          the food cost per portion
          the nutritional value of the dish   *p293*

2   an efficient costing system discloses the net profit made by each
     department and shows the cost of each meal produced, reveals
     possible sources of economy and can result in a more effective use
     of stores, labour and materials, provides information necessary for
     the formation of a sound price policy, provides cost records that
     provide and facilitate the speedy quotations for all special
     functions, enables the caterer to keep to a budget.   *p293*

3   overcooking food results in portion loss
     poor portion control
     too much wastage
     inaccurate ordering procedures
     inadequate controls   *p293*

4   a sound knowledge of all commodities   *p285*

5   compare quality with price   *p285*

6   keep up to date with prices, be aware of new products, have an
     efficient system of ordering, compare purchasing methods, keep
     number of suppliers to a minimum, request price lists, buy in
     season, check deliveries, invoices, statements, return containers,
     foster good relations with suppliers   *pp285–86*

7   false – price list must be up-to-date not out-of-date   *p285*

8   control of size or quantity of food served   *p287*

9   to ensure correct amounts are purchased   *p287*

10   true   *p287*

11   fair price for a fair portion   *p287*

12 type of customer, quality of the food, buying price of food   *p287*

13 scoops, ladles, individual pie dishes, moulds etc.
soup plates, glasses etc.   *p288*

14 4–6   *p288*

15 8   *p288*

16 16–24   *p289*

17 true   *p290*

18 4–6   *p290*

19 2   *p289*

20 primary – source of supply, grower, market
secondary – middle man, wholesaler
tertiary – retail or cash and carry   *p290*

21 detailed document of each commodity describing exactly what is
required.   *p291*

22 supplier knows what is wanted, storekeeper knows what is to be
supplied, assist costing and control procedures   *p291*

23 to ensure required quality, yield consistently   *p293*

24 prices fluctuate, customer requirements change, staff change   *p297*

25 uncooperative staff, difficulties with standardised recipes, incorrect
purchasing, large number of dishes, dishes with large number of
ingredients   *p297*

26 receiving, issuing   *pp297–98*

27 number of customers, what will be chosen from menu   *p300*

28 producing right amount of food, efficient preparation, good
portion control, utilisation of all foods, elimination of theft,
accurate ordering and checking, use of standardised recipes   *p300*

29 enables: efficient budgeting, analysis of the operation, shows where
improvements can be made   *p293*

30 false – systems need to be made to suit the establishment   *p294*

31 food, labour, overheads   *p294*

32 **a** variable costs
b fixed costs   *p294*

33 rent, uniform business rates, heating, lighting equipment, repairs, maintenance   *p294*

34 sales less food cost   *p295*

35 sales less total cost   *p295*

36 **a** gross or kitchen profit
     b net profit
     c sales   *p295*

37 selling price   *p294*

38 true   *p296*

39 it should do   *p296*

40 gross profit   *p295*

41 **a** a sound up-to-date knowledge of all items, awareness of what is available, be cost conscious, have an efficient system, create a suitable relationship with suppliers, purchase foods in season, check all deliveries, check all invoices, check all statements, keep abreast of new products and equipment, consider using computers   *pp285–86*
     b chef, manager, food and beverage manager, storekeeper, buyer or buying department
     c markets, cash and carry, suppliers – retail, wholesale   *pp290–91*

42 **a** controlling the size and/or quantity of food served to each customer
          i type of customer and establishment – male or female, age, fitness, kind of function, number of courses, how much is charged, kind of menu
          ii food – good yield – no waste, accurate means of portioning, individual portions
          iii price – good food – good price, fair portion – fair price, price to suit market
     b ice cream – scoop, soup – ladle and/or size of bowl, weighing each portion   *pp287–88*

43 **a** firstly define standard specification and standard recipe
          standard purchasing specification – exact description of every commodity detailing, as appropriate, grade, quality, size, weight, preparation, maturity, age, colour, shape etc.
          standard recipe – a precise formula for producing items of specified quality and quantity
          points to consider: all staff have same instructions, all

ingredients are consistent, therefore costing and control can be
effective at all times, variation of standards is eliminated

b inefficient storekeeper, inexperienced kitchen staff, lack of
supervision, inaccurate specifications   *pp291–92*

44 a assists planning, identifies variances, indicates net profit (if any)
by each section and cost of each meal, makes quotations
easier   *p293*

b staff co-operation, suitable system to establishment, clear
instructions to staff, staff training   *p294*

c food costs, labour costs, overheads
food costs – variable – varies according to business
labour costs – fixed costs – regular permanent staff, part time
staff – variable cost
direct labour costs – e.g. chefs, waiters (income from food)
indirect labour costs – managers, office staff, who work for all
departments
overheads, e.g. rent, heating, equipment, repairs, rates, lighting,
maintenance   *p294*

45 a price fluctuation, variation of transport costs, fuel cost rises,
food subsidies, changes in demand, media focus   *p297*

b menu changes, menus with large number of dishes, dishes with
large number of ingredients, problems of assessing demand,
incorrect use of standard recipes, incorrect purchasing,
incompetent staff, lack of supervision   *p297*

c purchasing, receiving, storing/issuing, preparing, selling
purchasing: obtaining foods and checking that purchasing
specifications are correct with regard to yield, enabling unit cost
to be known
receiving: checking to ensure goods delivered are in accord with
specification
storing/issuing: ensuring correct storage, decide method of
pricing so as to charge each department, e.g. actual price,
average price, fixed price etc.
preparation: number of meals produced, cost per meal
selling: predicting total number of customers, predicting menu
choice of customers, initial forecasting – final forecast *pp297–98*

d overcooking – portion loss, left-overs not utilised, inefficient
preparation – wastage, poor portion control, inaccurate
ordering, inaccurate checking, standardised recipes not used,
yield factors ignored, theft, unsuitable suppliers, bad menu
planning   *p300*

Purchasing

Read pp282–301 of *The Theory of Catering*.

QUESTIONS

1   Why is it essential to have a good working relationship with suppliers?

2   State three examples of labelling information provided on goods supplied.

3   Specify six important considerations in sequence when purchasing.

4   Name six points a purchaser needs to know regarding goods to be bought.

5   What is required of a supplier?

6   Describe
   a   Formal buying.
   b   Informal buying.

7   How may the three types of purchasing needs be divided?

8   List three points to be considered before purchasing.

ANSWERS

1   to ensure correct food safety and quality   *p282*

2   keep refrigerated, keep frozen, use by date, shelf life, best by date
                                                                             p282

3   know the market, decide purchasing needs, establish and use specifications, design purchasing procedures, receive and check goods, evaluate purchasing tasks   *p282*

4   where grown, seasons, costs, conditions of supply, regulations governing the products, marketing agents services, processing, storage requirement, class and grade of product   *p283*

5   ability to supply goods of the required quality in the required amounts, at the time needed   *p283*

6   a   informal buying – oral negotiations face to face or by telephone
   b   formal buying – written specifications and quantity needs   *p284*

7   perishable, staple, daily use   *p284*

8   number of people to be served
   record of past sales
   portion sizes   *p284*

Storekeeping

Read pp302–17 of *The Theory of Catering*.

QUESTIONS

1   A clean orderly food store run efficiently is essential in any catering establishment: true/false.

2   State three reasons for running an efficient food store.

3   Why is it desirable for a food store to face north?

4   Why is good ventilation and freedom from dampness essential in a food store?

5   State six points necessary for a well-planned store.

6   To maintain good standards of hygiene what is essential with regard to walls, ceilings and floors?

7   All store containers should be easy to clean and have tightly fitting lids: true/false.

8   Cleaning materials, because they have a strong smell, should be kept
>   on the lowest shelves in the store
>   on the highest shelves in the store
>   at one end of the store
>   in a separate store.

9   Name the three groups into which foods are divided for storage purposes.

10   What is the correct procedure with cases of tinned food?
>   Leave in the cases until required.
>   Open case at one end so that cans can easily be removed.
>   Unpack the cases and stack on shelves.
>   Unpack the tins, inspect them and then stack on shelves.

11   Why should dented tins be used as soon as possible?

12   Briefly describe the layout of an efficient vegetable store.

13   Name four qualities of a good storekeeper.

14   First in first out is a good rule for issuing stores: true/false.

15   What are requisitions?

16 Every time goods are received or issued, the appropriate entries should be made on both the stores ledger sheet and the bin card: true/false.

17 Explain the reason for your answer to the previous question.

18 What is a *departmental requisition book*?

19 An order book is filled in every time the storekeeper wishes to have goods delivered: true/false.

20 Is an order book in triplicate or duplicate?

21 Should all entries in the order book be signed?

22 If you answered yes to the previous question, who should sign the orders?
   manager, chef, storekeeper, finance officer

23 What is the purpose of the stock sheet?

24 Stock should be taken at regular intervals of
   one week or one month, two weeks or two months, three weeks or three months, four weeks or four months

25 What is the purpose of stock-taking?

26 What is a *spot check*?
   An inspection of food to see if germs or spots are present.
   A check of a few random items of stock.
   A check on the cleanliness of bin cards.
   A check on all bin card entries.

27 Delivery notes are sent with goods supplied as a means of c . . . g that everything ordered has been d . . . . d

28 What is the relationship between the delivery note and the duplicate order sheet?

29 Invoices are sent out to clients setting out the cost of the goods supplied or services rendered: true/false.

30 *Bill* is another name for an . . .

31 An invoice should be sent out
   on the day the goods are sent out
   one month after the goods are sent out
   two months after the goods are sent out
   six months after the goods are sent out.

32 What do the *terms of settlement* on a bill mean?

33 A credit note is issued stating (choose one)
>how much is owed to the company
>allowances made for adjustments and returnables
>how much credit the company allows
>allowance for staff meals.

34 Statements show (choose one)
>the state of the company at the half year
>details of the purchases of the quarter
>summaries of invoices and credit notes for the previous month
>amounts of goods returned during the month.

35 Give two examples of the use of credit notes.

36 When a client makes payment he or she usually pays by cheque. Will he or she also send back the statement?

37 Cash discount is discount allowed in consideration of p . . . payment.

38 Trade discount is discount allowed to whom?

39 *Gross price* is the price of an article before/after discount has been deducted?

40 *Net price* is the price of an article before/after discount has been deducted?

41 State four essentials for keeping a simple cash account.

42 Name a software package for computerising a store's control system.

43 **a** Explain why an efficient food store is essential in any catering establishment.
b State eight features which should be included in a well planned store.
c List six qualities for a good storekeeper.
d Explain the use of three documents used in the stores.

44 Describe the advantages of using a computer in a stores system.

ANSWERS

1   true   *p302*

2   stock available when required, prevents waste, record of who is supplied   *pp301–02*

3 avoids direct sunlight   *p302*

4 to prevent food spoilage e.g. by thus risking bacteria growth *p302*

5 well lit, easily cleaned, not cramped, working facilities, well
ventilated, conveniently sited, vermin proof, suitable counter *p302*

6 free from cracks, easily cleaned e.g. tiled floor and wall, rounded
corners   *p302*

7 true   *p303*

8 separate store   *p303*

9 perishable, non-perishable, frozen   *p304*

10 unpacked, inspected and stacked   *p304*

11 tin may rust   *p304*

12 cool, dry, well ventilated, bins for root vegetables, shelves for other
vegetables   *p309*

13 honest, organised, experienced, grasp of figures   *p309*

14 true   *p303*

15 list of items required from stores from departments   *p309*

16 true   *p311*

17 balance on both should be the same   *p311*

18 a book with details of goods ordered by the department from the
stores   *p311*

19 true   *p312*

20 duplicate   *p312*

21 yes   *p312*

22 storekeeper   *p312*

23 to record what stock is available   *p312*

24 weekly or monthly   *p312*

25 to check availability of stock, to prevent stealing   *p312*

26 a check of a few random items of stock   *p312*

27 checking that everything has been delivered   *p312*

28 a means of checking that which is ordered, is delivered   *p312*

29 true   *p312*

30 invoice   *p313*

31 day goods are sent out   *p313*

32 that discount may be given if account is settled by a specified
time   *p313*

33 allowances made for adjustments and returnables   *p313*

34 summarised invoices and credit notes for previous month   *p313*

35 overcharging, empty crates etc. returned   *p313*

36 yes   *p314*

37 prompt   *p314*

38 one trader to another trader   *p315*

39 before discount has been deducted   *p315*

40 after   *p315*

41 date entries, enter money received, from whom, on left or debit
side, enter money paid out, to whom, on right or credit side,
balance the account frequently   *p315*

42 catadata, XI data

43 **a** correct level of stock, items entering or leaving, a check can be
kept on each department's expenditure, waste can be
eliminated, hygiene can be maintained, safe for people working
there   *pp300–01*
b away from direct sunshine, well ventilated, free from dampness,
vermin proof, conveniently sited, have washing facilities, first aid
box, floors, walls and ceiling free from cracks and easily cleaned,
easily cleanable shelves, well lit, a suitable counter, weighing
machines, facilities for refrigeration, deep freeze, chill rooms
etc., steps and trolley   *p301*
c honesty, experience, knowledge of the stock, tidiness, a grasp of
figures, clear handwriting, a liking for the job, ability to get on
with people, a knowledge of computers is desirable   *p309*
d bin card, order book, requisition book, stores ledger, stock
sheets
e.g. bin card – a card for every item of stock showing: name of
commodity, issuing unit, date goods received or issued, from

whom received and to whom issued, maximum stock, minimum stock, quantity received, quantity issued, balanced held

pp310–15

44 streamlines operation, removes unnecessary manual paperwork, system automatically checks stock levels, adjusts costs and prices, provides necessary information when required, stock directly relates to recipe and menu requirements, system allows storekeeper or manager access to information quickly   *p496*

PROMOTION, SELLING AND CUSTOMER CARE

Read pp318–47 of *The Theory of Catering*.

Merchandising

Read pp320–3 of *The Theory of Catering*.

QUESTIONS

1 **a** Describe what is meant by merchandising.
   b Give an example of merchandising in catering.

2 Give three examples of how a caterer may display different items in order to make the product more attractive.

3 Merchandising requires space and strategic points that should be considered in order to give maximum effect. List four points which should be considered.

ANSWERS

1 **a** merchandising is the art of displaying products attractively to promote sales
   b in a fast food restaurant illustrated facia above the counter showing what is available with the help of colour photographs
                                                                        p320

2 the use of fresh flowers and fruits on display
   how the menu is displayed and the language used
   how food is displayed on a buffet table
   the use of finished dishes for display i.e. a selection of plated sweets
   on a tray   *p321*

3 customer flow
   entrances and exits
   use of displays outside restaurants
   position of check in and cash desks   *p321*

Service of food

Read pp323–38 of *The Theory of Catering*.

QUESTIONS

1   State four varied types of food service.

2   Which method of food service is the most expensive to operate?

3   Explain briefly why kitchen staff should appreciate the problems of waiting staff.

4   State four points to be considered for the benefit of both the waiter and the customer when plating or dishing food.

5   Which of the following establishments may use cafeteria service?
     works canteen; popular restaurant; first class hotel; hostel

6   Name the type of service where customers usually help themselves to the food.

7   Give four advantages of automatic vending.

8   State four examples of different foods served at speciality restaurants.

9   a Explain how an establishment could be promoted prior to opening.
     b What are the objectives of advertising? Suggest a suitable method for an advertising campaign for a hotel or restaurant.
     c Explain how in-house selling can increase sales.
     d How may sales be maintained or increased during the year?

10   State the kinds of service used and fully explain one of them.

ANSWERS

1   waiter or waitress, hatch or counter, buffet, cafeteria, bar service, take away   *p323*

2   waiter/waitress   *p323*

3   to provide the customer with good service, to enable the waiting staff to do this; by knowing the waiters' problems the kitchen staff can prevent or lessen them   *p323*

4   correct amount, even sized portions, easily served, pre-plated is not disturbed   *p323*

5   works canteen, popular restaurant, hostel, staff facilities in first class
    hotel   *p325*

6   buffet   *p326*

7   available 24 hours, limited staff required, tea breaks may not be
    needed, disposables eliminate clearing and washing up, available
    when customers require items   *p327*

8   e.g. pancakes, hamburgers, chicken, pizza

9   a define target population then make special effort to inform
      potential customers by mail and/or hand bills. Use media, local
      press and radio. Advertise outside the premises, etc.   *pp318–23*
    b to promote an establishment, to increase custom by making the
      premises known, to inform those unaware of what is available,
      to remind those of continued existence of establishment, etc.
      e.g. sell the capability of the staff, chef, waiter, manager,
      through the media, use the menu as a means of advertising in
      the press, concentrate campaign into a special week, use special
      menu and special dishes etc.   *pp318–23*
    c ensure waiting staff are encouraged to recommend dishes,
      trained waiting staff need to be knowledgeable regarding dishes'
      composition; in hotels, rooms would have menus and details of
      special events, reception staff should be knowledgeable of
      menus and dishes so as to suggest using facilities of the
      establishment, etc.   *p323*
    d constant high standard of both kitchen and waiting staff,
      avoidance of menu fatigue, ensure trends are not ignored,
      provide for all customers, e.g. vegetarian, decaffeinated coffee
      etc., do not neglect hygiene, etc.   *p323*

10 waiter or waitress, cafeteria, hatch or counter, snack bar, buffet,
    take away.
    cafeteria – popular restaurants, industrial canteens etc.,
    customer moves along counter and selects, served by counter
    hands and/or self service, collects cutlery, tables may be laid,
    customer or staff clear tables   *pp323–38*

Vending

QUESTIONS

1   Give six advantages of vending.

2   There are a number of points which should be considered when purchasing vending equipment. Give some examples of these points.

ANSWERS

1   refreshments available 24 hours a day   *p328*
    staff and labour costs are reduced
    consistency of quality
    control of stock, portion control and cash
    operating costs are lower
    space is better utilised
    hygiene control is maintained

2   cup capacity, ingredient capacity, number of selections, hygiene, extraction efficiency, ease of filling, reliability, drinks supply rate, servicing, availability of power   *p336*

Franchising

QUESTION

1   What is meant by franchising?

ANSWER

1   franchising is where a manager pays a licence fee and makes whatever he/she can above an agreed percentage on the food he/she sells   *p337*

Customer care

Read pp338–47 of *The Theory of Catering*.

QUESTIONS

1   Getting customers and keeping them creates revenue: true/false.

2   What is often the effect on a customer if the restaurant manager remembers their name?

3   'I'll take care of that for you right away.' This is a good example of a customer care phrase: true/false.

4   Why is good communication important within the organisation?

5   Why is it important to inform staff?

6   It is not important to define standards of performance: true/false.

7   What does body language tell us?

8   If a person has their arms folded what does this suggest?

9   How should eye contact be used in dealing with customers?

10 Define what is meant by stroking in customer care.

11 What is meant by pacing?

12 What is meant by being assertive?

13 State the main objectives of customer care.

14 In relation to customer care and the organisation you are working for, state what the staff must know.

15 Give examples of how a supervisor or manager can gain commitment from staff.

16 When dealing with customers, describe how staff should behave.

17 List examples of body language.

18 Why is it considered important to ask customers questions?

19 Give some advantages of assertive behaviour.

20 How should customer complaints be handled?

ANSWERS

1   true   *p339*

2   customers are often delighted   *p339*

3 true

4 good communication assists in the development of customer care
p341

5 so that they feel part of the organisation   *p341*

6 false; standards of performance must be monitored and measured
p341

7 body language tells us what people really mean; it is the art of seeing what others are thinking   *p348*

8 they are being defensive about something, they are cold, they are uncomfortable   *p348*

9 eye contact should be used as a way of acknowledging customers, making them feel welcome and as a foundation of building a good relationship   *p344*

10 stroking is giving any kind of attention   *p345*

11 pacing is speaking in a way that is compatible with your customers
p346

12 stating your views while showing that you understand their views, enhancing yourself without diminishing them, speaking calmly, sincerely and steadily   *p346*

13 putting the customer first
making them feel comfortable
making them feel good
making them feel important
making them want to return to your restaurant or establishment
pp338–47

14 what the company stands for
what is its mission
what behaviour the company values highly
that cutting costs is not more important than customer care
that all guarantees must be honoured
that the restaurant or establishment is in business to keep the customer happy
that happy customers can lead to repeat business and recommend actions to friends and colleagues   *pp338–47*

15 good leadership
avoiding unnecessary stress

seek ideas from staff on how to improve customer care
provide good customer care training
build pride in their work performance
provide constant update training on customer care   *pp338–47*

16 professional, understanding, patient, enthusiastic, confident,
    welcoming, helpful, polite, caring   *pp338–47*

17 appropriate dress, posture, movement, gestures, facial expressions,
    eye contact, eye movements   *pp338–47*

18 asking customers questions will demonstrate that you have
    understood what the customer wants, have the time to talk to
    them, consider the customer important, are able to find out how
    they feel, can keep control of the conversation, understand their
    needs and their complaints, know how to make customers feel
    better   *pp338–47*

19 gives you greater self confidence
    gives you greater self responsibility
    gives you greater self control, your mind is concentrated on
    achieving the behaviour you want
    can produce a win situation, opinions on both sides are given a fair
    hearing, so they feel that they have won

20 customers should be encouraged to complain on the spot; if they
    are unhappy about anything that is served to them, they should be
    encouraged to inform the member of staff who served them; this
    will give the establishment the opportunity to rectify the fault
    immediately; customers should be asked about their eating
    experience; the customer who complains should be treated well,
    they should be offered a free drink or meal; the complainant must
    become your ambassador, so show the empathy, use the
    appropriate body language, show concern and sympathise

KITCHEN PLANNING, ORGANISATION AND SUPERVISION

Read pp350–86 of *The Theory of Catering*.

Working methods

QUESTIONS

1 Outline some current trends in kitchen design in
   a hotels
   b banqueting
   c hospitals
   d industrial.

2 Give examples of equipment trends.

3 What should kitchen design consultants provide the caterer with?

4 The purpose of colour coding boards and equipment is to prevent cross contamination. Give an example of a colour coding system.

5 Place the following in order to show an efficient work flow when making croquette potatoes
      breadcrumbs, egg wash, flour, potato mixture.

6 Why is it desirable to have a planned layout when working?

7 Why is a place for everything and everything in place a rule worth following?

8 A skilled craftsman achieves a high standard of work with the
      least effort, most effort, great effort, considerable effort.

9 State three savings that can be made to reduce wastage by studying working methods.

10 In addition to paying attention to good working habits, it is desirable to (choose one)
      cultivate the right attitude to work
      to take 'short cuts' and finish early
      to work as fast as possible, irrespective of result
      to adopt an attitude of not accepting advice.

11 a Explain why a good method of work is desirable.
    b Give two examples of methodical working.
    c Describe four factors to be considered in a well planned kitchen, to enable a good work flow.
    d Who benefits, and how, by developing good working practices.

12 a What information is required before planning a kitchen?
    b How could one go about designing it?
    c What considerations need to be taken into account concerning
       i   Customers.
       ii Staff.
       iii Employers.
    d What ancillary departments may need to be considered when planning the kitchen?

ANSWERS

1 a hotels – greater use of buffet and self assisted service units
   b banqueting – move towards plated service, less traditional service
   c hospitals – greater emphasis on bought in frozen and chilled foods, reduced amount of on-site preparation and cooking
   d industrial – more zero subsidy staff restaurants, increased self service, for all items, introduction of cashless systems will enable multi-tenant office building to offer varying subsidy levels   *p357*

2 refrigeration, more concentration on providing CFC – free equipment, use of induction units, combination ovens, microwave and tunnel ovens, servery counters will be more decorative, environmental friendly equipment, water and energy conservation equipment   *p358*

3 consultants should provide the client with unbiased opinions and expertise not available in their own company; their aim should be to raise the standard provision, equipment installation, while providing an efficient food production operation which also takes into account staff welfare   *p358*

4 red for raw meat
   blue for raw fish
   brown for cooked meats
   green for vegetables
   white for general purposes
   yellow for sandwiches   *p360*

5   potato mixture, flour, egg wash, crumbs   *p363*

6   to save time and energy, increase efficiency, reduce wastage of
     space   *p361*

7   so that everyone knows where to find everything, thus preventing
     frayed tempers, wasted time and makes for a well-ordered kitchen

8   least effort   *p362*

9   time, energy, space   *p367*

10   cultivate the right attitude to work, e.g. positive, cooperative,
     willing, adaptable etc.   *p364*

11   **a** energy, time, hygiene, standards, job satisfaction, safety, waste,
          space   *p362*
     b e.g. crumbing: mixture, flour, egg wash, crumbs, reshape, tray,
          preparing runner beans   *p363–67*
     c no criss-crossing, back-tracking, equipment height, equipment
          siting, space, sequence   *p364*
     d employees – less tired, energy, time
          employer – efficient staff, contented staff
          customers – standards   *pp361–67*

12   **a** the legal requirements, environmental and building restrictions,
          monies available, menu, clientele numbers, space etc.   *pp352–56*
     b obtain architects, use squared paper, work to scale, view other
          establishments, use equipment manufacturers catalogues, use
          gas and electricity advisers etc.   *pp353–55*
     c i   customers: e.g. workflow to ensure quality without delay,
              minimum of noise, smell and heat, efficient equipment,
              hygienic
          ii staff: e.g. ventilation, space, hygienic, enough equipment,
              suitably sited, minimum walking etc.
          iii employers: e.g. designed to be efficient to produce satisfied
              staff and customers, low operational and maintenance costs,
              good utilisation of space etc.   *pp352–67*
     d wash up, stillroom, service area, stores, waste disposal etc.   *p352*

Kitchen organisation and supervision

1   What is the purpose of efficient kitchen organisation?

2   State four responsibilities of the head chef or head cook.

3   What is the French for the second chef?

4   A chef de partie is in charge of

> the food for small parties of customers
> a section of the work in the kitchen
> banquets, buffets and parties
> the menus for all functions.

5   In the traditional organisation what were the responsibilities of the larder chef, pastry chef, sauce chef and relief chef?

6   What does the word commis indicate?

7   What is the difference between a partie and a process system of kitchen organisation?

8   What is the name given to the chef responsible for the entrées?

9   Name four subsidiary departments of the kitchen.

10   What are the advantages of an operation where the kitchen is on full view to the customers?

11   What effect has the continually increasing costs of space, equipment, maintenance, fuel and labour had on the organisation of the kitchen?

12   The variety and number of dishes on the menu does not affect the organisation of the kitchen: true/false.

13   Give three examples of situations where large numbers of people need to be served food at the same time.

14   Good supervision is the effective use of: . . . , . . . and . . .

15   State the three functions of a supervisor.

16 As well as knowing how to do, what other quality does a supervisor need?

17 Give an example of why a supervisor needs to forecast and plan.

18 What should good organisation ensure?

19 Delegation is an important aspect of supervision: true/false.

20 A good supervisor
creates problems, makes problems, anticipates problems, causes problems.

21 Tick those qualities which an effective supervisor needs
good communicator, tactless, impetuous, possesses technical knowledge, organising ability, understanding of people, motivator, disciplinarian.

22 Give an example of the social influence of a supervisor.

23 State five elements of supervision.

24 **a** State four purposes of having an organised kitchen.
   b Describe four ways of achieving an organised kitchen.
   c Name and specify the duties of four parties in a large traditional kitchen brigade.
   d List four subsidiary departments of the kitchen and explain their function.

25 **a** State four qualities needed by a supervisor.
   b Specify the three functions of the supervisor's role and explain one.
   c What are the five elements or areas of supervision? Describe two of them.
   d In what way may a supervisor's responsibilities include understanding and caring for staff?

ANSWERS

1 production of correct quantity of food at the highest standard, on time, by most effective use of staff, equipment and materials   *p361*

2 organise staff, compile menus, order foodstuffs, produce required profit (or work within budget), engage and supervise staff, purchase equipment, be responsible for ancillary areas   *p375*

3 sous chef   *p375*

4 a selection of work   *p375*

5 larder – cold work, pastry – sweets and pastries,
sauce – entrées, relief chef – takes over on other chefs' days off
pp375–79

6 assistant *p377*

7 partie – system based on products, process – on methods of food production, processes wet and dry

8 saucier or sauce chef *p337*

9 scullery, stillroom, plate room, stores, china pantry, room service lifts *p380*

10 customers can see cleanliness of premises; staff know they are on view and work cleanly; stimulates customer interest

11 need for greater efficiency

12 false, usually the larger number of dishes requires staff to be more organised and efficient

13 banquets, school meals, hospitals, airlines *p361*

14 money, materials, manpower *p381*

15 technical, administrative, social *p381*

16 be able to do, as well as knowing how to do *p382*

17 so as to organise staff and materials to produce right amount of food on time *p382*

18 organising consists of ensuring that what is wanted is where it is wanted, when it is wanted, in the right amount, at the right time
p383

19 true *p384*

20 anticipates problems

21 a supervisor should *not* be tactless or impetuous

22 be interested and care so as to motivate and obtain co-operation of staff

23 forecasting and planning, organising, commanding, controlling, coordinating

24 **a** quality of food, quantity, economical, increases productivity and efficiency, on time, safety, hygiene etc., reduces labour costs.
p361

    b planning, staffing, buying, maintaining, supervising, system etc.

p361

    c choose from
       pastry, sauce, roast, vegetable, larder, fish sections
       e.g. sauce cook (saucier) cooks all the entrées i.e. meat,
       poultry and game (not roasts or grills), sauces and certain
       garnishes   *p375*

    d clerk, porters, scullery, stillroom, stores, plate/china room, food
    lift
       e.g. stillroom: preparation and service of beverages, bread,
       butter, rolls, afternoon teas   *p380*

25 **a** communicate, coordinate, organise, motivate, initiate, decide,
    inspire, mediate   *p381*

    b technical, administrative, social
       e.g. social: staff relationships – co-operation – motivate – control
       – organise   *p382*

    c forecasting/planning, organising, commanding, controlling,
    coordinating
       e.g. commanding: who, how, what, when, where, priorities,
       decisions   *p382*

    d free from fear, free from discrimination, feel wanted/valued,
    fair, encouraging, prevent problems, listen to problems, solve
    problems   *p385*

CATERING EQUIPMENT

Read pp387–422 of *The Theory of Catering*.

QUESTIONS

1   Kitchen equipment is expensive. List the main points to consider when purchasing kitchen equipment.

2   Why is the correct use, care and maintenance of kitchen equipment so important?

3   State five points which are important for the maintenance and care of kitchen equipment.

4   Does a forced air convection oven have any advantage over a normally heated oven?

5   Briefly explain your answer to the previous question.

6   What advantage does a combination convection and microwave cooker have over an ordinary microwave cooker?

7   Microwave is a method of cooking and heating food by using . . . power.

8   What must not be put in a microwave oven?

9   What is the chief advantage of cooking by microwave?

10 State two advantages of the induction cooker.

11 Which is the odd one, and why, in relation to microwave cookery? glassware, silverware, plastic container, paper container, earthenware, chinaware.

12 The bratt pan may be used for which different methods of cookery?

13 What other advantages has the bratt pan?

14 Why is the steam jacket boiler most suitable for cooking large quantities of food with a thickened content?

15 What is the purpose of the *cool zone* in a deep fat fryer?

16 How is heat controlled on deep fat fryers?

17 What is the purpose of the hot plate (hot cupboard?)

18 A bain-marie is used for (choose one)
    washing vegetables, basting meat, keeping food hot, pot washing.

19 A double sided or infra-red grill is suitable for a fast food operation: true/false.

20 Match the following.
    salamander   heat above and below
    grill   heat above
    contact grill   heat under

21 Match the following.
    stainless steel sink   general light purpose
    glazed earthenware sink   heavy pot wash
    galvanised iron sink   general purpose

22 On which of the following surfaces would you cut with a knife?
    wooden table, cutting board, stainless steel, marble.

23 Hot pans should be placed on a . . . on the table in order to protect the table surface.

24 List three points to observe when cleaning a butcher's block.

25 Name three factors that should influence the decision whether to use an item of mechanical equipment.

26 What should be done before loading potatoes into the potato peeler?

27 Name six examples of use of a food mixing machine.

28 What can be the effect of overloading the mincer attachment of a food mixing machine?

29 What is the greatest potential danger to a food handler when operating a food slicing or chopping machine?

30 List five power-driven machines described as dangerous.

31 Working instructions should be placed in a . . . position near the machines.

32 Why should a refrigerator door be opened as little as possible?

33 Defrosting a refrigerator is necessary in order to
    produce more ice cubes
    stop foods from freezing hard

provide a supply of distilled water
prevent overworking of the motor.

34 Food should be packed into the refrigerator in order to maximise its use: true/false.

35 Is a single temperature suitable for keeping all types of food safe and at peak condition?

36 Why is it important to locate refrigerators away from sources of intense heat, direct sunlight and barriers to air circulation?

37 Why is it important to allow air to circulate within a refrigerator?

38 When preparing to empty and clean out a refrigerator what is the first thing to be done?

39 Refrigerators should be thoroughly cleaned inside and out at least every
    2 months, 4 months, 6 months.

40 Defrosting a refrigerator is important because it helps equipment perform . . . and prevents a damaging build-up of . . .

41 List two signs of an imminent breakdown in a refrigerator.

42 What are the generally recognised requirements for hygienic washing up?

43 Name the three main types of dishwashing machines.

44 Food compactors are the most modern and hygienic method of waste disposal: true/false.

45 Almost every type of rubbish and swill can be finely ground down and rinsed down the drain by food waste disposers, but what are the two exceptions to this?

46 How would you prove an omelet pan?

47 Name four different types of frying pan.

48 What is a conical strainer used for?

49 When could a sieve be used upside down?

50 Which has sloping sides, a sauteuse or a sauté pan?

51 What are the advantages of copper equipment?

52 What are the disadvantages of copper equipment?

53 Copper pans are lined with tin: true/false.

54 Why should the use of metal spoons or whisks be avoided with aluminium pans?

55 Is water boiled in aluminium pans suitable for making tea?

56 What material is used extensively for making pans?

57 Non-stick pans are best cleaned with
   wire wool, kitchen paper, Brillo pad, cleaning powder.

58 What three points should be observed in order to prevent warping and splintering of cutting boards?

59 Name three materials from which piping bags are made.

60 a How may kitchen equipment be conveniently categorised?
   b Having obtained equipment explain how it should be looked after.
   c What should be considered when planning to install large equipment?

61 a Select two major items of large equipment and explain their use and maintenance.
   b Choose two materials used to produce small kitchen equipment; describe their use and maintenance.
   c Explain the care and use of power driven mechanical equipment. What safety factors must be observed?

ANSWERS _____

1 overall dimension, weight, fuel supply, capacity, maintenance, construction, appearance, ease of cleaning and spare parts   *p387*

2 safety reasons, expensive to purchase and replace, hygiene reasons
   p387

3 periodic checks, careful usage, follow makers' instructions, report faults, keep a log book, record dates of servicing and what has been done   *p387*

4 yes   *p388*

5 it reduces evaporation loss, minimises shrinkage   *p388*

6 colouration and texture of food   *p391*

7	high frequency power	*p390*
8	metal or aluminium foil	*p390*
9	speed	*p390*
10	energy saving, hygienic, fast, easy maintenance	*p391*
11	silverware, because it would damage the oven	*p390*
12	boiling, stewing, shallow frying, deep frying, braising	*p394*
13	can be tilted, easy to remove liquids, easy to clean and rinse	*p394*
14	food does not burn	*p394*
15	for food particles to sink without burning	*p397*
16	by a thermostatic control	*p397*
17	keeping items hot	*p398*
18	keeping food hot	*p398*
19	true	*p399*
20	salamander – heat above grill – heat below contact grill– both above and below	*p399*
21	stainless steel – general purpose galvanised – heavy pot wash earthenware – light purpose	*p400*
22	cutting board	*p400*
23	triangle	*p401*
24	scrape, do not use water, use common salt and scraper, keep dry	*p401*
25	it can save time, save energy, produce a good product	*p401*
26	turn on water and set machine in motion	*p402*
27	making pastry, cakes, mashing potatoes, whisking whites, mincing or chopping meat or vegetables	*pp402–05*
28	machine can be damaged	*p402*
29	machine must have stopped and equipment stopped before hand is placed into bowl	*p405*

30 mincers, bowl choppers, dough mixers, food mixers, slicers, chippers   *p401*

31 prominent   *p401*

32 to prevent warm air entering and cool air getting out

33 to prevent overworking of the motor   *p411*

34 true   *p410*

35 no, not all food needs the same temperature   *p410*

36 so as to prevent machine overworking   *p410*

37 to maintain cooling   *p410*

38 switch off power   *p410*

39 at least every 2 months   *p411*

40 efficiently, ice   *p412*

41 unusual noise, fluctuating temperatures, frequent stopping and starting, excessive frost build up   *p412*

42 good supply of hot water, temperature 60°C, followed by rinse at 82°C for one minute   *p412*

43 spray, brush, agitator   *p413*

44 true   *p413*

45 tins, cloth   *p413*

46 heating with oil, salt may be used   *p414*

47 omelet, frying, pancake, oval fish   *p414*

48 passing sauces and straining gravies   *p415*

49 to pass flour   *p415*

50 sauteuse   *p416*

51 good conductor, food less likely to burn   *p416*

52 very expensive, need retinning, tarnishes   *p416*

53 true   *p416*

54 cause foods to discolour   *p417*

55 no, tea would be grey coloured   *p417*

56 special stainless steel *p417*

57 paper *p417*

58 dry thoroughly, stand on end, do not use for heavy chopping *p419*

59 linen, nylon, plastic *p421*

60 **a** large equipment, mechanical, small and utensils
   b follow makers instructions, do not misuse, check regularly, record maintenance, maintain repair, have a system, instruct staff, supervise staff *p386*
   c flow of staff, flow of materials, sequence of goods in to finished dishes, wash up, lighting, ventilation, services *pp352–60*

61 **a** e.g. Bratt pans: versatile – shallow, deep frying, stewing, braising, boiling, large surface area, tilting – care needed, but generally safe, gas or electric
   minimum moving parts, can be soaked and boiled for cleaning *pp386–401*
   b copper: most pans lined with tin used for e.g. sautéing, sauces, boiling, moulds e.g. dariole, bombes etc. unlined e.g. for sugar boiling
   copper is very expensive, retinning is essential when needed, clean inside by soaking, thoroughly cleaning, rinsing and drying, outside clean with a paste, rinse and dry *pp412–19*
   c follow maker's instructions, only trained staff to use, only one person to operate, maintain regularly, record maintenance, before cleaning switch off and remove plug, clean machine and attachments, reassemble correctly *pp401–13*

CATERING SERVICES

Read pp423–50 of *The Theory of Catering*.

Gas

Read pp423–31 of *The Theory of Catering*.

QUESTIONS

1   Name the three methods of heat transfer and give an example of each.

2   In the calculation of gas bills how does British Gas state the calorific value?

3   What is the purpose of a thermostat?
    to ignite the main jet, to control the pilot, to admit the air, to control the temperature.

4   **a** The action of a rod-type thermostat depends on the fact that some metals expand more than others when heated: true/false.
    b The action of a liquid thermostat depends on the fact that a vapour expands when heated: true/false.

5   Does air rise on being heated?

6   For what reason would Calor Gas be used?

7   Give an example of when it is extensively used.

8   **a** Explain how heat is transferred by radiation, conduction and convection. State a method of cookery relating to each.
    b Describe how to read a gas meter and explain how to work out the cost. Give an example of both.

ANSWERS

1   radiation – grilling, conduction – boiling, convection – roasting and baking   *p423*

2   British Thermal Units per foot and megajoules per cubic metre   *p425*

3   control the temperature   *p427*

4   true for both rod and vapour   *p427*

5   yes

6   where British Gas is unable to supply gas *p427*

7   outdoor catering *p430*

8   **a** radiation – directly onto food – grilling
       conduction – through base of pan – boiling
       convection – around the oven – roasting
    b read the bottom four dials – if pointer is between 0–9 read 9
       (diagram p426), from the present reading deduct previous
       reading, multiply this by price per therm, add the standing
       charge, price per therm and standing charge are stated on the
       gas bill *pp428–29*

Electricity

Read pp431–9 of *The Theory of Catering*.

QUESTIONS

1   Which of the following are insulators?
       rubber, glass, metal, tap water, plastic, porcelain.

2   The pressure of flow of electricity is measured by . . .

3   The rate of flow of electrical current is measured by . . .

4   The resistance of wires to the passage of electricity is measured
    by . . .

5   To cut off the entire lighting or power circuit you would
       phone the Electricity Board
       pull out all plugs and turn out all lights
       pull down the main switch
       sever the wires at the meter.

6   What name is given to electricity supplied to the UK?

7   A fuse acts as a s . . . d . . .

8   Which of the following can cause blown fuses?
       Too many appliances plugged into a circuit.
       Using a 5 amp fuse on a lighting circuit.
       Plugging a fire into a light socket.
       Short circuit due to insulation failure.
       Switching off at the main suddenly.

9   When repairing a fuse the first thing to do is
      stand on a non-conductor, turn off the main switch, phone for
      the electrician, turn off the appliance, put on rubber gloves.

10   When wiring a 13amp plug, match the following.
      green/yellow   live
      brown   neutral
      blue   earth

11   What percentage of the total energy used in the UK each year is
      accounted for by the hotel and catering industry?
      0.3%, 1.3%, 2.3%, 3.0%, 3.3%.

12   Give two examples of energy wastage in the use of kitchen
      equipment.

13   Describe two examples of energy saving equipment.

14 a Explain the purpose of fuses and circuit breakers.
    b What may cause a blown fuse?
    c What procedure is taken to repair a fuse?
    d Compared to other fuels state the four advantages and two
       disadvantages electricity has with other fuels.

ANSWERS

1	all except tap water	*p431*
2	volts	*p431*
3	amperes	*p431*
4	ohms	*p432*
5	pull down main switch	*p432*
6	alternating current (AC)	*p431*
7	safety device	*p433*
8	too many appliances plugged into a circuit, plugging a fire into a light socket	*p433*
9	switch off main switch	*p433*
10	live – brown neutral – blue earth – green/yellow	*p434*

11   1.3%   *p437*

12   turning on heat before needed, turning up heat too much, not turning off or down heat when not required   *p438*

13   microwave ovens, high pressure steamers, induction cookers   *p438*

14   **a** safety device   *p432*
    b too many appliances; plugging a power appliance into lighting; insulation fault   *p434*
    c turn off main; find blown fuse; remove; replace with new wire or correct cartridge; find and trace fault, repair then switch on *p434*
    d *Advantages*

Advantages	*Disadvantages*
clean	time taken to reheat
controllable	initial cost
labour saving	maintenance cost
good atmosphere	utensils
little heat loss	
no storage	*p437*

Water

Read pp439–50 of *The Theory of Catering.*

QUESTIONS

1   Name four things wholesome water is free from.

2   What are temporary and permanent hardness caused by?

3   A water company's stopcock is situated
    in the cistern, inside the premises, in the roof, outside the premises.

4   The *stop-cock* is also called the
    ball-valve, stop-valve, stop-pipe.

5   What is the purpose of a u bend and a p or s trap

6   Why is descaling necessary?

7   When water freezes it . . .

8   What is the reaon for lagging water-pipes?

9   **a** What do you understand by soft and hard water?

    b How may water be treated in catering establishments to soften water?

    c Give an example of how a caterer will benefit from having a water softener.

ANSWERS

1   suspended matter, colour, taste, harmful bacteria, mineral matter injurious to health   *p439*

2   temporary – calcium or magnesium carbohydrates
permanent – chlorides of calcium or magnesium   *p444*

3   outside the premises   *p440*

4   stop valve   *p442*

5   to prevent penetration of smells and airborne bacteria into kitchens etc.   *p447*

6   to ensure efficiency of and extend life of equipment   *p445*

7   expands   *p446*

8   to prevent water in pipe freezing   *p446*

9   **a** soft – mildly acidic; lathers easily
       hard – chalk: temporary – calcium dissolved in water
       permanent – chlorides and magnesium dissolved in water
    b water softeners – by chemical action
       descaling – by specialists using acid
    c tea and coffee boilers: reduces or eliminates need for descaling, increases life of boiler, reduces maintenance cost, increases flow of water   *p444*

CATERING SYSTEMS

Read pp451–95 of *The Theory of Catering.*

QUESTIONS

1 What is the primary objective of a hygiene committee?

2 What does HACCP stand for?

3 What is the purpose of a food hygiene audit?

4 Give the characteristics of a fast food system.

5 The term for reheating cook-chill food is
   regeneration, renovation, remuneration, restoration.

6 What is the difference between making sauces for cook-freeze and those for cook-chill?

7 When several kitchens are supplied from a main kitchen for heating frozen foods, they are called
   peramateur, peripheral, spherical.

8 List eight benefits of a cook-chill/cook-freeze system.

9 State four advantages of cook-chill over cook-freeze.

10 What is the most important factor to be considered with either system?

11 What is the function of a bacteriologist or microbiologist?

12 Describe the pouches used for sous-vide.

13 State four advantages and four disadvantages of the sous-vide system.

14 What is a *centralised production unit?*

15 What kinds of staff are required in a central food production system?

16 a Name two food production systems.
    b Explain four problems experienced in the industry that these systems are expected to help solve.
    c What is the top priority of any system and what must be observed?

    d Explain one food production system, giving specific times and temperatures where appropriate.

    e Explain the benefits to both employer and consumer of a food system.

17 Give examples of critical control points.

18 State what you understand by JIT relating to production planning of inflight catering.

19 Outline the principles of JIT.

20 State what you understand by the assembly kitchen concept.

ANSWERS

1 focus attention on the subject of food safety   *p452*

2 Hazard Analysis and Critical Control Point (HACCP)   *p452*

3 food hygiene audits are intended to scrutinise the food production operation with a view to recording deficiencies and areas for improvement   *p455*

4 fast food is characterised by a smooth operation with short queuing time   *p481*

5 regeneration   *p460*

6 modified starches are used to prevent water separation on reheating   *p469*

7 peripheral   *p470*

8 reduced waste, portions controlled, no over production, bulk purchase, equipment fully used, staff time fully used, saving on space, fuel and equipment, better staff conditions, less frequent deliveries   *p476*

9 regeneration simpler, no thawing time, less storage space, cheaper to run, blast chillers cheaper to install and run, cooking techniques unaltered, all foods can be chilled   *p476*

10 hygiene   *p452*

11 to check food is and will be safe to eat   *p470*

12 made of plastic for individual portions   *p477*

13 advantages – long shelf life, no risk of cross contamination, reduced labour costs, full flavours of food retained, inexpensive reheat disadvantages – cost of pouches and machine, not suitable for all dishes, not suitable for complete meals, twice conventional cooking time required *p478*

14 a kitchen for producing cook-freeze or cook-chill supplying one or more regeneration sites *pp478–82*

15 machine operators; trimmers; packers; staff trained on the premises *p480*

16 **a** cook-chill, cook-freeze, sous-vide *p451*
  b staffing, food, equipment, energy, overheads, space *p451*
  c hygiene: stringent hygiene, prevention of infection, separation of raw/cooked, consultation, thorough cleaning, strict control of time/temperature, staff training *pp452–58*
  d e.g. cook-chill: food cooked correctly, chilling within 30 minutes, chilled to 3°C within 1½ hours, store between 0°C–3°C, distribute minimum temperature, regenerate immediately to min 70°C, consume within 2 hours *pp458–67*
  e employer: control, purchasing, number of staff, no unsocial hours, waste, equipment, space, delivery, production, staff time, fuel consumer: variety, quality, nutrition, constant *p476*

17 inspection, temperature checks on goods delivery and before use, separate storage and handling of ingredients and the finished product, correct temperature ranges, cleaning procedures for equipment and utensils, personal hygiene and health standards, proficiency in use and cleaning of equipment *pp451–95*

18 producing the necessary units in the necessary quantities at the necessary time *pp451–95*

19 stock levels are kept down to the level when required, ordered in when needed (stockless production), elimination of waste, enforced problem solving, continuous flow manufacturing *pp451–95*

20 it requires a thorough understanding of how to switch over from the traditional labour intensive production method to a more industrial type of production; the concept includes preparing the food component in an appropriate kitchen, respecting the legislation, arranging everything cold (even raw) on to the plate, regenerating (even cooking) on the same plate as served *pp451–95*

COMPUTERS IN CATERING

Read pp496–506 of *The Theory of Catering*.

QUESTIONS

1 What benefit is there in using computers?

2 Describe hardware and software.

3 What are the two types of software?

4 Briefly explain the two types of software.

5 Name examples where computers can be used in food and beverage situations.

6 What is the purpose of a spreadsheet?

7 Why is a database valuable?

8 IT and VDU are initials for what?

9 What is the intention of the Screen Display Regulations 1992?

ANSWERS

1 they provide reliable, up to date information   *p500*

2 hardware is the physical equipment; software is the instructions which the computer understands   *p500*

3 system software and application software   *p500*

4 systems software is usually fitted with windows and a mouse as an input device; applications software performs tasks e.g. stock control   *p501*

5 stock control, recipes, menus, diets   *p502*

6 deals with numerical data   *p505*

7 it stores on file information, graphics, etc.   *p505*

8 information technology, visual display unit   *p509*

9 to safeguard the health of VDU users   *p509*

HEALTH
AND SAFETY

Read pp508–29 of *The Theory of Catering*.

QUESTIONS

1   What do the initials COSHH stand for?

2   State the labels used to describe dangerous substances.

3   What items used in the kitchen could come into the category of harmful?

4   Briefly state the two aims of the Health and Safety at Work Act.

5   At work every employee must take reasonable care of himself or herself and who else?

6   Regarding safety at work, an employee must not interfere with what?

7   An employee should co-operate with whom at all times?

8   Whose function is it to improve the existing standards of hygiene, to act as an adviser and to enforce the hygiene laws?

9   State three ways in which accidents can be caused in the kitchen.

10 During a busy kitchen service, the golden rule is 'never run': true/false.

11 Why may a blunt knife be more likely to cause an accident than a sharp one?

12 State five safety rules to be observed when handling knives.

13 What is the most important safety precaution to observe when cleaning a cutting machine?

14 Why should guards be in place when using machines?
    To do the work more quickly.
    To prevent the operator being injured.
    To deter stealing.
    To stop food being spilled.

15 Why should frozen meat be thawed before being boned?

16   If you cut your hand with a fish bone it may turn s . . .

17   What is a burn caused by?

18   What is a scald caused by?

19   When an accident occurs who must be informed?
     the police, the hospital, the employer, the health officer.

20   The sensible length to wear an apron in the kitchen is
     ankle length, just below the crutch, just below the knees, under
     the arms and around the waist.

21   Explain why, when working over the stove, it is sensible to have
     the jacket/overall sleeves rolled up or down?

22   State three essential points for an oven cloth.

23   When shallow frying, in which direction is the food put into the
     pan and why?

24   What must be to hand when foods are tipped out of the frying pan
     into the friture? Explain why.

25   To warn that the handle or lid of a pan is HOT would you
     write on it the word hot in flour
     place a piece of red paper on it
     put the burn ointment beside it
     sprinkle a little flour on it.

26   The correct amount of fat in a movable friture for safety purposes
     is
     ⅔ full, ½ full, ¼ full, ¾ full.

27   What should be done to wet foods before deep frying them?

28   Should the fat in a movable friture bubble over on to a gas stove,
     you would first
     call your immediate superior
     call the kitchen porter
     lift out the food with a spider
     turn off the heat source.

29   When using a mixture machine with a blade, whisk or hook, what
     is the essential safety precaution that you should observe?

30   State five safety rules to be observed when using machinery.

31 A gas explosion can be caused in the kitchen because
  there is no pilot
  the gas is turned off at the main
  the main jet has not ignited from the pilot
  the gas has not been turned on.

32 It is not necessary to mop up water spilt on to a kitchen floor as the heat of the kitchen will do this fairly quickly: true/false.

33 Why should containers containing liquid never be put above eye-level?
  Other persons not aware that they contain liquid.
  Liquid above eye-level is difficult to control.
  Containers above eye-level are heavier.
  Liquid in the container moves more when above eye-level.

34 State four signs indicating that a person is suffering from shock.

35 What is the first-aid treatment for a cut?
  Sprinkle it with salt in order to disinfect it.
  Give a glass of brandy.
  Wash the skin around the cut and apply a waterproof dressing.
  Wrap it in a tea-towel and send for the doctor.

36 If breathing has stopped what must be started before any other treatment is given?

37 Slight burns or scalds should be immersed in
  iced water, warm or cool water, hot running water, cold running water.

38 In cases of electric shock, firstly
  give the person a glass of water, switch off the current, apply artificial respiration, send for a doctor.

39 State three signs which may indicate a person is about to faint.

40 Name a common cause of fire in a catering establishment.

41 List the correct procedures in the event of a fire in the kitchen.

42 If a fire is spreading in the kitchen, what should be done to doors and windows?

43 Match the appropriate extinguisher with the type of fire.
  fire blanket   fire caused by fat
  foam   electrical fire
  dry powder   person's clothing on fire

44 Fuel and heat are two sides of the fire triangle, what is the third side?

45 To remove the fuel is to . . . the fire.
To remove the air is to . . . the fire.
To remove the heat is to . . . the fire.

46 Match these colours to types of fire extinguishers
blue, red, green, black, cream.

47 **a** State the main aims of the 1974 Health and Safety at Work Act.
 b What three health and safety responsibilities has an employee?
 c Specify three actions the Health and Safety inspector and EHO can take.

48 **a** Explain how a worker's attitude to safety can prevent accidents.
 b Which accidents must be reported?
 c What information must be recorded in an Accident Book?
 d List the accidents most likely to occur. Explain four rules to prevent injury from knives. Explain four rules to prevent injury from burns and scalds.

49 **a** List items contained in a first aid box.
 b What is the treatment for burns and scalds?
 c What is the first aid for cuts?
 d Which organisations run first aid courses?

50 **a** List the procedure in the event of fire.
 b Name two pieces of equipment other than portable extinguishers, to put out fires.
 c Explain and give examples why the correct extinguisher must be used for specific fires.

ANSWERS

1	control of substances hazardous to health	*p508*
2	very toxic, toxic harmful, irritant, corrosive	*p508*
3	some cleaning materials	*p509*
4	extend protection of law to all employees and employers, increase awareness of safety at work for both employers and employees	*p509*
5	other persons at work	*p509*

6 anything provided in the interests of health, safety or welfare *p509*

7 his or her employer regarding health and safety *p509*

8 Environmental Health Officer *p574*

9 excess haste, distraction, failure to apply safety rules *p515*

10 true *p515*

11 because excess pressure needs to be used

12 use correct knife, do not place in sink, when carrying, keep point down, keep handles clean, place knives flat on table or board, keep knives sharp *p515*

13 make sure machine is unplugged *p518*

14 to prevent operator being injured *p516*

15 difficult to handle, hands become cold, knife slips easily *p516*

16 septic *p516*

17 dry heat *p516*

18 wet heat *p516*

19 employer *p514*

20 just below the knees *p517*

21 down, to protect the arm from heat of the stove and splashes of liquid *p517*

22 thick, dry, not torn *p517*

23 away from the person so that no splashes go towards the person *p518*

24 spider – to lift out foods quickly if needed *p518*

25 sprinkle with a little flour *p517*

26 ⅔ full *p518*

27 drained and dried *p518*

28 turn off the heat source *p518*

29 hands must not be placed inside bowl until whisk etc. has stopped *p518*

30 machine must be in working order, only one person at a time to

operate machine, use only correct attachments for specific purposes, do not place hands in bowl when still in motion, remove plugs before cleaning   *p518*

31 main jet has not ignited from pilot   *p518*

32 false – immediately mop up spillage   *p519*

33 other persons not aware that they contain liquid   *p519*

34 faintness, sickness, clammy skin, pale face   *p521*

35 wash and apply waterproof dressing   *p521*

36 artificial respiration   *p522*

37 warm or cool water   *p522*

38 switch off current   *p522*

39 whiteness, giddiness, sweating   *p521*

40 deep fat fire   *p523*

41 call fire brigade, do not panic, warn others in vicinity, do not jeopardise safety of self or others, follow fire instructions, use appropriate fire extinguisher for small fire, close doors, windows, turn off gas, electricity and fans   *p524*

42 close them   *p524*

43 fire blanket – person's clothing
foam – fat fire
dry powder – electrical   *p525*

44 oxygen   *p522*

45 starve, smother, cool   *p523*

46 blue – all purpose powder
black – CO_2 gas
red – water
green – halons
cream – foam   *p524*

47 **a** Legally protect all employers and employees, increase awareness of safety   *p509*
b take reasonable care of him/herself and others, comply with requirements, not misuse or interfere   *p509*
c prohibition notice, improvement notice, prosecute, seize goods
                                                                        p514

48 **a** avoid haste, distraction, follow safety rules   *p514*
  b all accidents, also those involving dangerous machinery   *p515*
  c e.g. name, occupation, supervisor, time and date of accident and report, nature of injury, extent of injury, evidence of person, treatment, place of accident, witnesses   *p516*
  d cuts, falls, burns, scalds
     cuts: correct knife, sharp, clean, laid flat, not in sinks, point down
     burns: sleeves, thick cloth, balance trays, pan handles, roux, caramel, frying, steamer doors   *pp514–19*

49 **a** first aid information, waterproof dressing, cotton wool, dressings, scissors, safety pins, triangular bandages, eye pads, tweezers, report book   *p520*
  b cool/cold water, ten minutes, clean cloth/dressing, if serious, hospital, *no* ointments etc.   *p522*
  c wash, cover, direct pressure, hospital, if serious   *p521*
  d St Johns Ambulance Association, British Red Cross   *p522*

50 **a** call fire brigade, do not panic, warn others, follow instructions, use appropriate extinguisher, close doors etc.   *p524*
  b hoses, fire blankets
  c water conducts electricity, foam conducts electricity, halon not a conductor, carbon dioxide not a conductor, water and foam not effective when electricity is cause of fire   *p525*

HYGIENE

Read pp529–72 of *The Theory of Catering*.

Personal hygiene

Read pp529–34 of *The Theory of Catering*.

QUESTIONS

1   S . . . respect is necessary in every food handler.

2   Personal cleanliness is essential to prevent g . . . getting on to food.

3   Give another word for *germs*.

4   When particularly must hands be thoroughly washed?

5   Why is jewellery not worn in the kitchen?

6   When handling food you should use
      flesh-coloured nail varnish, pink nail varnish, no nail varnish.

7   Why should finger nails be kept short when handling food?

8   Why should the hair of kitchen staff be covered?

9   When handling food, hair should be covered (choose from)
      because of the appearance of the worker
      because of the legal requirements
      to keep customers happy
      because of hygienic reasons.

10 Why are paper handkerchiefs or tissues preferable to linen or cotton handkerchiefs?

11 Why is it important not to sneeze over people, food or working surfaces?

12 Sound teeth are essential to good health: true/false.

13 You should visit the dentist
      every 5 years, every 3 years, every 6 months, when you have toothache.

14 When tasting food which should you use?
      wooden spoon, teaspoon, your finger, ladle.

15 Where on a person's head will large numbers of bacteria be found?

16 Cuts, burns, scratches and similar openings in the skin are best covered with
clean gauze, clean bandage, waterproof dressing, antiseptic ointment.

17 Explain two ways in which germs may be transferred on to food by someone smoking in the kitchen.

18 Spitting is an objectionable habit which should never occur, but why is this?

19 Where should outdoor clothing, and other clothing which has been taken off before wearing whites, be kept?

20 How frequently should kitchen whites be changed?

21 List four essential points to ensure good health and physical fitness.

22 When working in a hot kitchen and perspiring freely, the ideal way to replace liquid lost is by
taking salt tablets, taking glucose tablets, drinking pure water, drinking beer.

23 Why should picking of food be discouraged?

24 Match the following important points for kitchen clothing:
protective   to be comfortable in a hot atmosphere
washable   to enable perspiration to be soaked up
suitable colour   need to withstand hard wear
lightweight   to indicate the need to be washed
strong   because of the need for frequent change
absorbent   to prevent excess heat affecting the body

25 Why should only healthy people handle food?

26 To which three groups of people is kitchen hygiene particularly important?

27 **a** Explain why personal hygiene is essential and describe how it is achieved.
b Explain the purpose of protective clothing and state five points the clothing should fulfil.

28 The Food Safety Act 1990 has increased the powers of whom?

29 The Amendments of the Food Hygiene Regulations 1995 relate to what?

30 At what temperature should hot foods be kept above?

ANSWERS

1	self respect	*p529*
2	germs	*p529*
3	bacteria	*p529*
4	after visiting the toilet	*p529*
5	may drop into food, may prevent proper washing of hands, particles of food may lodge under rings	*p530*
6	not use nail varnish	*p530*
7	less easy for dirt to lodge under nail, easier to clean	*p530*
8	to prevent hair or drandruff getting into food	*p530*
9	for hygienic reasons	
10	because they are thrown away, thus cannot harbour germs	*p531*
11	to prevent germs being spread	*p531*
12	true	*p531*
13	six months	*p531*
14	a teaspoon which should be washed after every use	*p531*
15	nostrils, ears, mouth	*p531*
16	waterproof dressing	*p531*
17	by contact with fingers and mouth, by contact with cigarette end that has been in the mouth and put down on working surface	*p531*
18	because of spreading bacteria	*p532*
19	in a locker away from the kitchen	*p532*
20	as often as necessary to ensure hygienic conditions – aprons at least daily, twice or more if needed	
21	fresh air, food, water, exercise, rest	*p532*
22	drinking pure water	*p532*
23	it becomes a habit and spoils the appetite	*p532*
24	protective – protects body from heat and spillage washable – needs frequent washing	

colour – indicates need for washing
lightweight – comfortable
strong – hard wearing
absorbent – soaks up perspiration   *p533*

25 because of the possibility of conveying to others ill health via
food   *p534*

26 employees, employers, customers   *p535*

27 **a** protects from germs, self respect, fitness, good health,
cleanliness of body, care of cuts, clothing, cosmetics,
smoking   *p531*
b to protect food, the worker
washable, light in weight, strong, colour, comfortable,
absorbent   *p533*

28 Environmental Health Officers   *p542*

29 Temperatures of food in transit, in store and in preparation
production and service   *p567*

30 63°C or 115°F   *p567*

Kitchen hygiene

Read pp534–42 of *The Theory of Catering.*

QUESTIONS

1 Windows in the kitchen used for ventilation should be screened to
prevent the entry of dust, insects and birds: true/false.

2 State five important factors of kitchen wall surfaces.

3 Name three items of kitchen equipment which are difficult to clean
and state how you would clean them.

4 When cleaning large equipment such as electrical mixers, slicers
etc. what should be done first?

5 Failure to maintain equipment and utensils hygienically and in
good repair may cause food . . .

6 Why should you not wash aluminium saucepans in water
containing soda?

7 Why should tinned, lined saucepans be dried after being washed?

8   Give a definition of hygiene.

9   Number in order of importance.
   Having the right attitude to hygiene.
   Seeing films on hygiene.
   Reading books on hygiene.
   Practising hygienic habits.
   Attending lectures on hygiene.

10   Food handlers should not only know the Food Hygiene Regulations, but should practise them in their daily work: true/false.

11   In a catering establishment can any of the following be excused in relation to hygiene?
   Neglect, ignorance, thoughtlessness, low standard, poor facilities.

12   The average number of notified cases of food poisoning each year over the past ten years has been
   5,000, 10,000, 15,000, 20,000.

13   **a** Explain why a kitchen should be hygienic.
   b State five essential items of cleaning equipment and explain the procedure to ensure their supply.
   c State four particular items or parts of the kitchen to be kept clean. Describe in detail how one of them is cleaned.
   d What area must never be cleaned by food handlers?

14   **a** State four points enabling equipment to be easily cleaned.
   b Sieves and conical strainers are difficult to clean. Describe the way to clean them.
   c List the sequence for cleaning large electrical equipment.

ANSWERS

1   true   *p535*

2   free from cracks, flaking, light in colour, smooth, strong, impervious   *p536*

3   e.g. sieve, and conical strainer – under fast running water and moving up and down in a sink of water
   whisks – clean thoroughly where wires cross over and clean the whisk handle   *p539*

4   remove electric plug   *p540*

5	poisoning	*p538*
6	soda may affect protective film	*p539*
7	possibility of rusting if not dried	*p539*
8	study of health and prevention of disease	*p543*
9	right attitude, practising hygiene, books, lectures, films	*p543*
10	true	*p543*
11	no	*p543*
12	20,000	*p543*

13 **a** employees benefit – working conditions clean, employers benefit – more customers, consumers benefit – know premises/staff clean *p535*

b brooms, buckets, cloths, cleaning materials, dustbins, cleaning machine etc.
budget – order – store – issue *p535*

c ventilation, floors, ceilings, lifts, lighting, walls, windows
e.g. floor: swept, washed, dried, mechanical/hand, safety *p535*

d toilets *p536*

14 **a** no ridges, screws, ornaments, dents, crevices, square corners *p539*

b spray tap water, bristle brush, shake up and down in sink *p539*

c switch off, remove plug, remove food particles, clean, hot detergent water, rinse, dry, reassemble, test *p540*

Food hygiene

Read pp542–64 of *The Theory of Catering.*

QUESTIONS

1 What is *food poisoning*?

2 List eight ways to prevent food poisoning.

3 By far the greatest number of cases of food poisoning are caused by harmful . . .

4 How may food be contaminated?

5 What have the following in common?
zinc, rhubarb leaves, lead, arsenic.

6   By what means can chemical food poisoning be avoided?

7   What word means the same as *poison*?

8   What can bacteria, which forms spores, withstand for a long time?

9   Because bacteria multiply by dividing in two under suitable conditions, one bacterium could multiply in 10 to 12 hours to between:
100,000–200,000, 400,000–500,000,
100,000,000–200,000,000, 500,000,000–1,000,000,000.

10   Typhoid, paratyphoid and dysentery are known as f . . . b . . . diseases.

11   For the multiplication of bacteria what four conditions are necessary?

12   Are bacteria killed by cold?

13   Name four foods most easily contaminated.

14   In which of the following should food not be stored and why?
larder, refrigerator, store, kitchen.

15   Why should food be kept in a cool larder or refrigerator?

16   Which of the following provides an ideal heat for bacteria to grow?
cold soup, hot soup, lukewarm soup, boiling soup.

17   State the temperatures between which bacteria multiply rapidly.

18   Will bacteria remain dormant for long periods?

19   If foods have been contaminated before being made cold and kept in the refrigerator, on raising the temperature by keeping the foods in the kitchen for a period of time the bacteria will . . .

20   Bacteria require moisture for growth, they cannot multiply on dry food: true/false.

21   State four dishes ideal for growth of bacteria.

22   Indicate the foods which need the greatest care to prevent food poisoning.
gravy, cream, milk, tea leaves, dried peas, aspic, jelly, flour.

23   *Salmonella* is the name of
a patent fly catcher
the scientist who discovered food poisoning
living, food poisoning bacteria
an insect spray fitted in kitchens.

24 Where are staphylococci present?

25 Explain the danger to humans of flies landing on food.

26 What is meant by cross contamination?

27 Germs present on human hands and other parts of the skin and in the nose or throat or sores and spots are s . . .

28 Name the three places food poisoning bacteria live.

29 What two things must be done to bacteria to prevent food poisoning?

30 With what type of food poisoning are cats, ducks, flies and insects associated?

31 What is the responsibility of the carrier of an infectious disease?

32 Indicate how infection can be spread by
     humans, animals, insects, birds, inanimate objects.

33 The cook's best friend in the kitchen is a cat or small dog as they will help to kill the rats and mice. Discuss briefly.

34 State six ways to prevent infestation from vermin.

35 What conditions are liked by cockroaches?

36 When cleaning pans used for porridge or starchy foods they should initially be
     soaked in cold water, soaked in warm water, soaked in salt water, soaked in hot water.

37 The temperature of washing up water should be
     67°C, 77°C, 87°C, 97°C.

38 In which months of the year is extra care needed when storing foods?

39 Which kind of meat joints need extra care in cooking? State why.

40 Why may some shell fish, such as oysters and mussels, cause food poisoning?

41 Which sauce made with eggs is liable to cause food poisoning? Describe briefly how this can happen, and what precautions can be taken.

42 *Rechauffé* indicates what kind of dish?

43 Milk, to be safe should be
     pasteurised, pacified, pasturised, patronised.

44 Name four made-up food dishes that require extra care in their preparation.

45 Tinned hams should be stored in the refrigerator: true/false.

46 Why should boned and rolled joints of meat require extra care in cooking?

47 Pork should always be well cooked: true/false.

48 Explain the reason for your answer to the previous question.

49 Why do made-up dishes require special care and attention?

50 Why must watercress be thoroughly washed?

51 When handling left-over foods for re-use, if in doubt as to their freshness, what golden rule should you follow?

52 What are the two temperature controls for food storage?

53 List two items which should be available near to hand basins in kitchens?

54 Where can copies of the Food Safety Act Regulations be obtained?

55 What is the penalty for any person found guilty of an offence under the Food Safety Act Regulations?

56 Name two institutions concerned with health and hygiene.

57 **a** State three reasons why food poisoning may occur.
b List ten ways food poisoning can be prevented.
c What causes food poisoning?
d State three ways to prevent chemical food poisoning.

58 **a** What are the characteristics of bacteria?
b State the four conditions for bacterial growth.
c List the foods requiring extra care.
d Take two of the conditions stated in answer (b) and explain in detail.

59 **a** State the three most common food poisoning bacteria.
b Briefly describe each of the most common forms.
c What are the sources of food poisoning?
d How can food poisoning be prevented?

60 **a** Animals, insects and birds can bring infection into food premises, explain how one of these three groups do this.
b Explain six points of importance concerning washing pots and

pans and three points concerning washing crockery and cutlery.
 c List six foods requiring special care.
 d What is meant by the following in relation to food hygiene
     reheated dishes, cross contamination, food-borne diseases.

61 **a** Food hygiene regulations apply to most catering establishments.
     What do the regulations require regarding
        equipment, personal requirements, premises.
   b What may an environmental health office check for? Compile a
     check-list to cover hygiene and safety.

ANSWERS

1 an illness caused by eating affected food   *p545*

2 high standard of personal hygiene, physical fitness, good working
   conditions, equipment clean/repaired, cleaning facilities, correct
   storage of foods, correct reheating of foods, correct cooling of
   foods, eliminate vermin and insects, hygienic washing up, food
   handlers knowing how to prevent food poisoning and practising
   prevention   *p545*

3 bacteria   *p545*

4 by chemicals and germs   *p545*

5 all poisonous   *p545*

6 using correct utensils, obtaining food from reliable sources, care in
   use of poisons   *p546*

7 toxins   *p545*

8 heat for long periods of time   *p547*

9 500,000,000–1,000,000,000   *p548*

10 food-borne   *p548*

11 food of a certain kind, suitable temperature, adequate moisture,
    time   *p549*

12 no, they are dormant   *p550*

13 e.g. milk products, sauces, made up dishes, reheated dishes   *p552*

14 kitchen, because it is too hot for storage   *p549*

15 low temperature prevents multiplication of bacteria *p549*

16 lukewarm soup *p549*

17 10°C–63°C *p549*

18 yes *p549*

19 multiply *p549*

20 true *p550*

21 e.g. trifle, cottage pie, hollandaise sauce, jelly *p550*

22 gravy, cream, milk, jelly, aspic *p550*

23 living food poisoning bacteria *pp551–52*

24 human hands, skin, sores, nose and throat *p554*

25 transfer germs from contaminated places *p556*

26 the conveying of germs from raw to cooked foods or cooked to raw by hands, boards, utensils etc. *p553*

27 staphylococci *p554*

28 the soil, humans, animals *p554*

29 stop bacteria multiplying and spreading *p555*

30 Salmonella *p553*

31 to inform the person responsible for the premises *p555*

32 human – coughing, sneezing, by hands
animals – hair, droppings
inanimate – dirty tea towels, dishcloths, boards, knives *pp555–61*

33 they should not be allowed in food premises as they can carry harmful bacteria on their coats, local council can be called in to get rid of rats *p557*

34 building in good repair, no rubbish to accumulate, premises kept clean, tight fitting lids on dust and swill bins, no food left about, stock moved to check signs of vermin *pp555–58*

35 warm, moist, dark places *p558*

36 soak in cold water *p560*

37 77°C *p560*

38 summer months *p561*

39 boned and rolled, as inside may have been contaminated *p562*

40 they may have been bred in containated water *p563*

41 hollandaise – if made in the morning and kept warm and used in the evening bacteria could multiply *p563*

42 reheated *p563*

43 pasteurised *p563*

44 fish cakes, cottage pie, fish pie, home-made mousse *pp563–64*

45 true *p562*

46 because of the possibility of contamination during preparation in handling *p562*

47 true *p562*

48 because of the possibility that tape worm may enter body *p562*

49 because time between original cooking and re-use and the extra handling may enable bacteria to multiply or food to become contaminated *p563*

51 throw it out *p563*

52 8°C, 45°F and 5°C, 41°F *p567*

53 soap, nailbrush *p566*

54 HM Stationery Office

55 heavy fine or imprisonment

56 Royal Society of Health, Royal Institute of Public Health and Hygiene *p571*

57 **a** ignorance, carelessness, thoughtlessness, equipment, cleaning facilities, accident, checking suppliers premises and transport and supplies *p545*
b personal hygiene, physical fitness, work conditions, maintenance, cleaning equipment, storage, reheating, cooling, vermin/insects, washing up, staff *p545*
c chemicals, bacteria *p546*
d correct utensils, maintained utensils, foods from reliable sources, care in use of rat poison etc. *p546*

58 a everywhere, immobile, transferred, produce toxins, multiply in body/in food, some useful, food poisoning, other diseases, need air/no air   *p547*

  b food, temperature, time, moisture   *p552*

  c stocks, sauces etc., meat, meat products, milk, milk products, eggs, egg products, handled, reheated foods   *p548*

  d e.g. temperature: growth rapid between 10°C–63°C, refrigeration, freezing, washing up, boiling water, time, weather, body temperature   *p548*

59 a Salmonella, Staphylococcus aureus, Clostridium perfringens*p566*

  b e.g. Staphylococci aureus; humans: hands etc., sores, cuts, spots, nose, throat; handled foods; other foods often affected   *p548*

  c soil

  humans – intenstines, nose, throat, skin

  animals – insects, birds, intestines, skin

  d prevent multiplying and spreading

  humans – coughing, sneezing etc.

  animals – droppings, hair etc.

  objects – towels, dishcloths, knives, boards etc.   *p554*

60 a e.g. birds: enter premises, to prevent entry, how they contaminate   *p555*

  b soaking, scraping, washing in hot water, change frequently, rinsed, storing

  remove, scrape, wash, hot detergent water, clean water, air dry, temperature, machine wash with clean brushes   *p560*

  c made-up, pork, handled meat, fish, watercress, reheated, poultry, sausages, milk   *p561*

  d reheated dishes: sound food, thorough reheating to 98°C for 10 minutes, quickly reheated

  cross contamination: raw – cooked foods must not come into contact through use of same knives, boards etc., hands must be thoroughly cleaned, storage of raw and cooked foods separate

  food borne diseases: typhoid, paratyphoid, scarlet fever, tuberculosis, dysentery, listeria

  carriers: water, milk   *p563*

61 a equipment: clean, repaired   *p569*

  personal requirements: clean person, clothes, cuts, spitting, smoking

  premises: toilets, washing facilities, lighting/ventilation, sleeping rooms, first aid, lockers, refuse, food temperatures and storage   *p569*

b hygiene: grease, dirt, pests, staff toilets – clothing, hazards, records, cracked equipment, storage – provision, temperature, notices, supervision   *p569*
safety exits – fire escapes, fire equipment, lighting, water supply, ventilation, hand washing, soap, nailbrush, towel, flooring, walls, ceiling, equipment – instructions, guards, training, clothing, storage, refuse   *p561*

Food hygiene regulations

Read pp564–9 of *The Theory of Catering*.

QUESTIONS

1   At what temperature must all hot foods be kept above?

2   Name two foods which must be kept below 5°C (41°F).

3   State two items of food to be kept at under 8°C (46°F).

4   Are sterilised and pasteurised canned foods exempt from temperature control?

ANSWERS

1   63°C (115°F)   *p568*

2   e.g. smoked fish and meat, and segments of ripe soft cheese   *p568*

3   e.g. dairy based desserts and prepared salads   *p568*

4   sterilised cans are, pasteurised cans are not   *p567*

INDUSTRIAL RELATIONS

Read pp573–8 of *The Theory of Catering*.

QUESTIONS

1   Effective relationships in industry depend on
    a Cooperation between . . . and . . .
    b Knowing . . . passed by Parliament.
    c Having the . . . towards the laws.

2   List six reasons why good industrial relations are not easy to create
    in the catering industry.

3   Very briefly state the purpose of a trade union.

4   What function should the shop stewards perform?

5   What should the Sex Discrimination Act prevent?

6   Who does the Race Relation Act help?

7   What is the meaning of the word *discrimination*?

8   The Equal Pay Act specifies that equal pay is paid to whom?

9   When assessing people for employment what considerations must
    not affect the issue?

10 The Employment Act is concerned, among other things, with the
    dismissal of staff. Give two fair and two unfair grounds for
    dismissal.

11 What do the following initials stand for?
    AGM, AOB.

12 What is an *agenda*?

13 A written record of committee decisions is termed . . .

14 Why would a person be *out of order*?

15 Briefly explain
    ex-officio, status quo, quorum.

16 When all present at a meeting vote for the motion it is said to
    be . . .

17 A vote in favour of a motion is said to be . . .

18 **a** State three essentials for effective industrial relations.
    b List the legislation which affects the industry and explain the implications of one of the Acts.
    c What is the purpose of a trade union? Name one to which catering staff belong.

ANSWERS

1   **a** employer and employee
    b laws
    c right attitude   *p572*

2   labour turnover high, majority of establishments are small, few employers union minded, not just one union involved with the industry, many foreign employees not English speaking, many part-time workers, many seasonal jobs, unsocial hours, industry has poor image   *p572*

3   to look after interests of their members at work e.g. hours of work, conditions and pay   *p574*

4   present the member's grievance to superiors   *p574*

5   female employees being treated less fairly than male employees
                                                                         p575

6   persons of a different race   *p576*

7   unfair treatment of persons of a particular race, religion or social group etc.   *p576*

8   males and females   *p575*

9   the person's race, religion, gender, being a trade union member
                                                                   pp575–76

10 fair – incompetence, genuine redundancy, misconduct, foreigner with no work permit
    unfair – unfair selection for redundancy, being or proposing to be a union member   *p576*

11 Annual General Meeting, Any Other Business   *p577*

12 list of items to be discussed   *p577*

13 the minutes   *p577*

14 by not conforming to the rules or conduct of the meeting   *p578*

15 *ex officio* – because of his or her office, e.g. person in the chair of
an organisation is a member of all its committees
status quo – return to the original situation
quorum – minimum number of members required to be present
pp576–78

16 unanimous   *p578*

17 carried

18 **a** cooperation, employer-employee, knowing legislation, right
attitude to legislation   *p572*
  b equal pay, trade union and labour relations, employment
protection, sex discrimination, race relations, health and safety
at work
e.g. Equal Pay Act – same for men and women doing the same
work, graded competence, experience   *p574*
  c interest of members at work, pay, conditions and hours of work.
Transport and General Workers, General and Municipal
Workers

GUIDE TO STUDY AND EMPLOYMENT

Read pp579–89 of *The Theory of Catering*.

QUESTIONS

1   What is the name of the comprehensive record an employee or potential employee may send to an employer?

2   When applying for a job, the names of two people may be required to act as
      umpires, referees, judges.

3   State six qualities an employer may look for in a good prospective employee.

4   In which publication may you find advertisements for jobs in the catering industry?

5   What must never be written on a job application?

6   Which of the following should you take when going for an interview?
      Any certificates you possess.
      Your mother, or close relative.
      The address of where the interview is to be held.
      The telephone number of the potential employer.
      Any questions you may wish to ask.
      A bottle of wine as a gift.

7   At an interview which is the most important?
      To be clean, neat and to sit up and not smoke.
      To be clean, neat but if nervous to ask for a light for a cigarette.
      To lounge but be clean and tidy.
      To be over-confident, ask many questions, be clean.

8   Should you not obtain the job, state three reasons why you may have been rejected.

9   Besides money, what do you want from employment in the catering industry?

10 How may you remedy any shortcoming regarding your own employability?

11 What are the four levels of NVQ or SVQ?

12 What is understood by APL?

13 State four reasons why entering competitions may be beneficial.

14 Regarding any competition it is essential to read and understand the . . .

ANSWERS _____

1   CV (curriculum vitae)   *p585*

2   referees   *p585*

3   punctuality, appearance, speak up, knowledge of company, attitude to catering, experience if appropriate or willingness to learn

4   *Caterer and Hotelkeeper*

5   untruths   *p586*

6   certificates (if any), address of where interview is, telephone number of potential employer, any questions   *p586*

7   be clean, neat, sit up, not smoke   *p586*

8   other applicants more suitable, interviewed badly, not what employer wanted   *p587*

9   consider job satisfaction, interesting work, experience, like the people   *p587*

10 assess your ability, experience, attitude, how you interview, how you get on with others, how nervous you may be; by attending more interviews and remedying any shortcomings you have assessed, you should succeed; ask friends and tutors for advice   *p587*

11 operative, craft, supervisory, junior or mid management

12 Accreditation of Prior Learning; credit is given for previous knowledge and experience

13 experience, opportunity to learn, to compare with others, to improve

14 rules